The Magic of Unknowing

An East-West Soliloquy

The Magic of Unknowing

An East-West Soliloquy

Mervyn Sprung

broadview press

BROADVIEW PRESS
Peterborough, Ontario, Canada

Founded in 1985, Broadview Press is a fully independent academic publishing house owned by approximately twenty-five shareholders—almost all of whom are either Broadview employees or Broadview authors. Broadview is supported by a collaboration with Trent University, a liberal arts university located in Peterborough, Ontario—the city where Broadview was founded and continues to operate. Broadview is committed to environmentally responsible publishing and fair business practices.

Library and Archives Canada Cataloguing in Publication

Sprung, Mervyn
The Magic of Unknowing: An East-West Soliloquy
ISBN 0-921149-08-5
1. Philosophy. 2. Rationalism. 3. Knowledge, Theory of. I. Title.
B995.S73M34 1987 121 C87-093479-1

Broadview Press handles its own distribution in Canada and the United States:
PO Box 1243, Peterborough, Ontario K9J 7H5, Canada
555 Riverwalk Parkway, Tonawanda, NY 14150, USA
Tel: (705) 482-5915
email: customerservice@broadviewpress.com

Broadview Press books are imported and distributed in the United Kingdom and European Union by:
Gazelle Book Services Ltd.
White Cross Mills, Hightown, Lancaster, Lancashire, LA1 4XS
sales@gazellebookservices.co.uk

European Union – Responsible Person (for official use only):
eucomply OÜ
Pärnu mnt 139b14
11317 Tallinn, Estonia
hello@eucompliancepartner.com
+33757690241

Broadview Press acknowledges the financial support of the Government of Canada for our publishing activities.

Canada

Broadview Press® is the registered trademark of Broadview Press Inc.

PRINTED IN CANADA

4 5 6 7 8 9 10 26 27 28 29 30

MIX
Paper | Supporting responsible forestry
FSC® C013916
FSC www.fsc.org

The interior of this book is printed on 100% recycled paper.

The Soliloquy

Afternoon

Erosion From Within

The Storm

Assault From Without

After the Storm

Metamorphosis

Evening
The Magic of Unknowing

The author acknowledges assistance from the Social Sciences and Humanities Research Council of Canada in the writing of this book; and from the Canadian Federation of the Humanities, using funds provided by the Social Sciences and Humanities Research Council of Canada, in its publication.

Afternoon
Erosion From Within

Aristos of Gnosis

One late summer afternoon, sensing his end near, the aging philosopher Aristos of Gnosis gathered around him in the cool warmth of the great maple tree overlooking the lake those of his many sons who had proved least receptive of his scientific understanding of the world and once again, and for the last time, sought to instruct them in his philosophy. Seated in the family circle were the son from Elis, the oldest, born of untamed Artemis, and René born of the blessed St. Sophia, and David born of a bonnie Mary; close by was Immanuel born of a wise valkyrie and, just slightly apart, leaning against a great stone was Friedrich born of a fierce maenad; next to him reclined Ludwig, the youngest of the brothers, born of the judicial lady Linguistica, only faintly interested in the family council. By his side and so completing the circle sat two foster sons lately arrived, Chang from the land of the ancients, in his black robe and cap, and Nagaraj from the land of the *sadhu*, composed in his lotus seat.

Aristos, erect and benign for his many sons, stepped into the circle and, standing, began his teaching, "My sons, I have summoned you to a family council this afternoon because each of you has revealed to me in quiet talk how deeply bitten you are by the virus of scepticism, and how deeply you question the sovereignty of science. Well and good; but take heed. Scepticism, though it brings a heady sense of power, especially to young men, is in the end debilitating, for its induces to nihilism. Nothing can come of philosophy if its faith in the sovereign power of knowledge is destroyed. You are thoughtful and learned beyond your years; but I lay upon you the need to study the world as it is before indulging in your personal speculations.

"Bear in mind that the real world is made up of physical objects, from our own bodies to the most distant stars, all arrayed predictably in cosmic space. We are acquainted with the surface aspects of these objects through our senses – tasting, seeing and so on – but it is the mind, our cognizing faculty, which probes their inner nature and gives us what we call knowledge, the sustenance of human life. The scientific mind explores and masters the incessant processes among objects and their elementary particles, ascertaining their highest causes, and so is able to predict the behaviour of things.

"True, some important laws are still to be discovered, but with what we know at the present time we can explain and predict most events that happen around us. We know the nuclear secrets of nature and how it is that men can walk in space. Whatever the forces and elements still unknown to us, science will, by always turning to the world of things, succeed eventually in mastering them. The areas of human ignorance will gradually narrow and perhaps in time will be eliminated wholly, for the human mind is capable of knowing all things. Knowledge of first principles is *sophia*, the highest knowledge, and our pursuit of it is philosophia. To philosophize is to understand all things through knowledge. I have never been able to agree, as you all know, with my great teacher, he of the broad shoulders, that humans are most in need of knowledge about a supposed world of invisible things – truth, beauty, goodness and the like – which can be explored by thought alone without the use of the senses.

"In the course of inconceivable time a myriad of living species has evolved on this planet, including the most complex of all, ourselves. As humans we have a capacity for feeling and a powerful array of instincts like earlier species but, unlike earlier species, we are gifted with reason. Reason is our sovereign faculty. If there is anything divine in the world it is knowledge of the ultimate causes of things. Each of us develops personal preferences in what is good and bad, beautiful and ugly; growing out of these preferences, each of us, aided by reasoning, shapes his life toward the realization of his ambitions, for death ends our adventure.

"But scientific knowledge is not limited to the physical and biological behaviour of things and animals. Science has no less the responsibility of discovering the laws governing the subjective world of personal attitudes and values, the surfaces and depths of the psyche, and as well the laws governing people in their societies. Only as science succeeds in this will we be able to plan a human society duly ordered in harmony with these laws. We – I should of course say "you" – must assemble all the scientific talent we can to master the nature of all things, human and non-human. On this will depend the ability of you and your descendants in the long future ahead to evolve a world society which ensures, in justice, equal freedom to all humans."

Aristos paused and looked affectionately and, it seemed, with a hint of commiseration into the faces of his sons seated around him. "I will leave you now," he said, "so that you may think on what I have told you and talk about these great matters among yourselves. Let my last word to you be this. If you find you cannot accept what I have taught you – above all the sovereign value of scientific knowledge – you must prepare yourselves to live with the momentous consequence. Either you find another principle of equal power and beneficence on which to secure the future of the human species, or you will be delivered over to the darkness of instinctual powers. May you grasp the momentousness of this fateful turn in human affairs and may the gods attend you in your thinking." With measured, rythmic movements the great man stepped out of the circle of his sceptical sons, walked across the field, and turned back into his mansion.

René

René, the youngest of the brothers, laid aside his beads and spoke up impetuously. "Much as I revere our aged father," he began, "I am driven by the twin convictions that the sciences in our time must be founded on a sharper understanding of their own methods than they were in his day, and that the conduct of our own lives is in need of a single principle secured by the light of reason. The science of our father seems to me to lack a centre, a unifying principle, and so to be adrift both in its claims and in its application to our personal lives. The Christian church can teach us the truths of religion, but we must ourselves think out their rational foundation and the way they should enter into the conduct of our lives. If we can succeed in finding this rational principle – and I can now tell you all that I believe I have succeeded –" René's excited eyes glanced at the faces around him, "then man can become the master of nature and enjoy all her treasures. As all of you, except our new foster brothers, know well I believe, we must begin by stripping ourselves of all opinions and beliefs pressed on us by our teachers and our books, all ancient learning, and so free the natural light of reason that is in everyone. It will be our guide."

René paused for breath and looked quickly around the seated circle. Though the brothers had often argued these questions, they had never before subjected one another to formal statements of their views. All except Ludwig appeared to be quizzically interested; he doodled with pencil and paper. Chang, under his pointed black cap and Nagaraj, under his shiny monk's head were motionless, but their bodies, strained slightly forward, betrayed an absorption in the momentous encounter.

"I am no sceptic," René went on, "as our eldest brother is. His pyrrhonistic views fulfil Aristos' prophecy. They undermine science and lend themselves to a nihilistic life-view. I have discovered, though, that it is through doubting everything that we can possibly doubt, that is, everything that we can imagine to be other than the way we believe it to be, that our reason is freed to secure what is certain knowledge. In the long afternoons this summer I have been carrying out exercises to test this. I have told myself that I will accept as certain, as beyond doubt, only what, by the way it presents itself to my mind, is *self*-evidently what it presents itself to be.

"You can try this yourselves. We all know that the senses of sight, hearing, taste and so on can, very often do, and in some cases must deceive us. Sounds can be heard as coming from the wrong direction; the voice of Immanuel can be mistaken for Ludwig's; objects at a distance are seen as smaller than when close by, the rising and setting sun and moon as larger than when on high; warm water is hotter on the elbow than on the face, and so on. So, as I have now come to think, we must doubt the existence of an ordered external world, simply because we *can* doubt it.

"But one's body is part of that world. If we doubt that our own bodily perceptions give us the truth about it, then we must suspect as well the feelings that we can have only through our body. Are our pains and pleasures true reports of the nature of things around us? As our consciousness itself can flicker and deceive – think how memory can falsify even the intimate, how our calculations can seem right but be erroneous, how our perception of friends and enemies can be distorted – we can and must doubt whether our everyday awareness is not a dream consciousness, whether all the things it claims to be aware of really exist, whether the whole of life itself isn't a kind of moving picture, a dream.

"In this way I push doubt to its farthest limits. We must doubt until we have found something in our lives, in ourselves, that, by its nature, makes doubting impossible, that is, something that does not point to or rest on something else, but only to and on itself. Some experience, some clarity must strike us which can *only* be what one takes it to be, something so self-evidently standing in virtue of its own nature that its truth is given with itself and is free of the possibility of error.

"Now I want to tell you that in my meditations of this past summer I have discovered what is certain beyond doubt, the bedrock of my new rational science. It came about this way. It struck me suddenly that in my very doubting, even as I tried to find all things false, it was, in reason, incontrovertible that the 'I' who had been doubting, this very 'I' that, in the moment in which it doubted realized it was engaged in doubting, had to be *something*. It could not be an illusion because it presented itself without anything intervening between it and the awareness of it. It was *self*-certain, *self*-evident. With a leap in my heart I saw that my discovery 'Because I *doubt* I must exist,' or, as I now prefer to put it, 'Because I *think* I must exist' was so assured that all the extravagant arguments advanced by the sceptics were incapable of shaking it. I knew that I could accept this truth, which I now offer to you as 'I think, therefore I am,' as the first principle of philosophy for which I have been searching. I knew further, and only today have I the courage to admit this, that my method was more certain and more useful than the law of contradiction in reasoning, the principle established so long ago by our father. You see, I may hold many assertions together in one argument or theory without any one contradicting any other, and yet be guilty of some error of reasoning. I can and I must always doubt the truth of statements merely because they agree among themselves. In my discovery, certain knowledge comes from absolute doubt, not from the absence of contradiction. Even my own existence becomes certain in the very act of doubting it.

"In this way it is now clear in the light of reason that the 'I' so encountered is a pure thinking being not dependent on a theory for its existence. This is philosophy's proof of the existence of the soul, hitherto assured us only by religious truth. Now reason can go further in its own natural light. I asked myself how it could be that I, an imperfect being – I am speaking of course for all human beings – could come by the idea of a perfect being outside of all created natural things: the Christian God. Such an idea could not derive from anything less than a perfect being, for nothing can be caused by what is less than itself. It must follow then that the idea of a being possessing all perfections could have been implanted in me by no other agency than such a being himself. So I have proved that God exists, or rather, reason has shown that God must exist. Even as the mere idea of a sphere implies, by definition, that every point on its surface is equally distant from its centre, so the mere idea of God implies, by definition, that God exists.

"This much is not only clear and distinct. It is furthermore true, because the light of reason which perceives clarity and distinctness is the light of God in us. If we were not sure of that, no amount of careful reasoning could assure us that our conclusions were true. But because we can be sure of that we can rest assured that what our reason tells us about the necessary nature of all things, including the external world, can be accepted as true. We can now be sure that the external world is made up of bodies extended in space, quite devoid of consciousness and soul and obedient to the mathematical laws of mechanics, which are the laws of God. Everything outside of the human spirit is thus to be understood in terms of soul-less mechanical laws. This is my discovery. I intend now to move forward into the realms of mathematics and nature, taking only such careful steps as are clear and indubitable in the light of what reason has established beforehand.

"What strange trajectories our thinking traces! I began by giving scepsis free flight, and this perturbed our father. But it was scepsis itself, pursued to its end, that yielded a fresh foundation for both science and morals in our time. We may now be sure that natural reason vouchsafes us certain knowledge. Aristos foresaw our time prophetically.

"Now you know, my brothers," René concluded, "what I have been doing much of the time you thought I was praying in the chapel. In any case, you can see how much, in spirit, I support our father's scientific faith. I did find it imperative, though, to build a more certain foundation for knowledge than he had done. That is why I turned my thoughts inward toward the discovery of the subjective basis for the principle of reason, and why I insist that without certainty of God's good intentions toward us we could have no confidence in the order of nature or in our ability to know that order.

"I know I am the youngest except for Ludwig, and I suppose a little brash to speak out so impetuously. I crave your indulgence, but with it your sober study of what I have said.

"Now I can see that Immanuel, who has had more time than I have had to think about our father's philosophy, is impatient to gain your ears."

René smiled good naturedly, settled back and took up his beads again while he turned to watch his older brother.

Immanuel

Immanuel laid aside the leather-covered volume of pietistic aphorisms he had been fingering and with a friendly nod acknowledged René. "Bravo, young man," he began in his engaging academic lisp, "You have gone deep in your meditations, deeper than anyone I have yet listened to. You have just given us a defence of reason in human affairs and the sciences, and a defence of the Christian religion by means of reason, that is classic. I say, all honour to you. You have challenged us all to re-examine our own beliefs. Indeed we can now do no other than express our beliefs in terms either of an agreement with or a criticism of your own principles. If you will permit me, I think that is exactly what I would like to try to do."

No one under the tree moved or spoke, though the brother from Elis cocked his close-cropped head quizzically to one side, Friedrich brushed his moustaches impatiently, and Ludwig bent over his sketches more intently. Immanuel began. "René's position, strong as it is, may nonetheless have the seeds of confusion in it. He is, as I understand him, justifying our knowledge of the physical world and our knowledge of the spiritual order, especially of God, by means of one and the same method of reasoning. This is, as I said, a classic thrust, but is it not open to abuse? In the first place, I can see those inclined to religious dogmatism falling into interminable disputes about the ultimate truths because they will believe that reason alone can produce from her great treasure all the arguments and proofs needed to establish the existence and attributes of divinity. Their squabbles will in themselves bring such disrepute down on the noble head of metaphysics that the undertakings of reason may, in all other branches of science, be thoroughly discredited. Worse still will be the effect of such disputes on the religious faith of Christians everywhere. Argument will eat away at the capacity of the faithful to sustain belief in their church and their God. Faith will become irrelevant.

"I see another possible result of René's thinking, potentially more disastrous than the first. If, as he has just told us, the infallible reason that is effective in securing truth in mathematics and the sciences of the physical world is the same reason that assures us of God's existence and attributes, then – this is my concern – will the physical scientists not be justified in applying their kind of knowledge and their methods of proof to spiritual matters? If they do – and how could they stop short? – can we doubt that, in the end, God will either vanish because He will be undiscoverable within the laws of the sciences, or else He will somehow be transformed into a secular principle within scientific reasoning?

"Because such misgivings have been much with me I have meditated deeply in my own heart on other ways of securing the moral and religious beliefs of men. I should better say, I have meditated on ways of securing for men the possibility of moral and religious truths and their right to believe in them – in their God, in the invaluable worth of human persons, in their own immortality. My thinking has been moving toward a way of showing that men have a suprasensible nature with its own laws, which is quite untouched by the order of physical nature. After a painful struggle I have concluded that so long as we believe that René's reason, the only faculty of cognition humans have, is authorized to range throughout a single universe obligingly ordered in conformity to it – as I think our father and René do believe – I, for my part, would find it neither possible nor meaningful to speak of a moral and religious realm existing apart from the scientific.

"The problem, in this age of swiftly advancing physical science, is the difference between the ability of the sciences to predict quite accurately the motions of the stars and the consequences of biological experimentation – in other words to establish laws of behaviour within the order of nature – and our inability to do this within the sphere of morals and religion. This is a plain fact that confronts us. If it were true that there is one all-inclusive order of things, this difference would be inexplicable. Indeed the scientist would be quite justified in holding that religious and moral aspirations, not being anywhere discoverable within his universe, were unreal, a confusion of thought, an illusion. For my own part I cannot believe that the noble history of mankind allows such a cynical conclusion.

"So I have tried to think of it this way. There must be some decisive difference in the way our reason is correlated to the world science knows and the way it is correlated to the world of religion and morals. I set myself the task of discovering this difference, and this afternoon in this fateful council – fateful because for the first time confronting the philosophies of our family with great thinkers from across the oceans – I am emboldened to put before you the conclusions I have arrived at. I must expect they will shock you as they at first shocked me.

"I began by looking again at what we mean by knowledge. We have always assumed that our knowledge must conform to the laws of the external world. Knowledge, we commonly believe, depends on there being concepts in men's minds that correspond to the structures of things quite independent of the mind, as they are in themselves, as it were. Now if this were the true state of affairs we would clearly have as precise knowledge of God's nature as we have of the stars. But we don't. So some great jolt to our thinking is needed if we are to come to terms with this conundrum.

"What if the relationship between the concepts we have of known things and the things known were turned around, if the dependence between concept and thing were reversed? I mean, suppose knowledge was not a matter of our concepts conforming to things, as we have always believed, but – and this is the new idea I am almost afraid of – of things conforming to our concepts? I am trying to make plausible the implausible notion that our mathematical and causal knowledge of processes in nature describes only that aspect of such processes which happens to fit our human concepts. It is not knowledge of nature as it might be quite apart from our specifically human way of grasping things. If we store up in our fund of knowledge only those processes which can be determined in our mathematical and causal reckoning, then we can comprehend how it is possible for science to predict, to a very great extent, the future course of precisely those physical processes. And we can comprehend how there might well be some other order of things which does not conform to our categories and concepts and so remains forever withdrawn from human knowledge.

"My new way of understanding the human situation – sometimes I call it, perhaps immodestly, my Copernican revolution – makes quite intelligible how it is that we can predict the exact time and place of a solar eclipse, but not know anything with certainty about God, the human soul, moral laws or any of the other mighty problems of metaphysics. The explanation is very simply that what we call an eclipse is an aspect of nature which conforms to our mathematics and to our concept of an event. God and the human soul do not.

"There is more. I believe I have discovered not only that knowledge, whether scientific or everyday, is possible only when what is to be known conforms to our human way of conceiving things, but also that it is possible only when it is *perceived* in our particular way. For us all perceptions must unroll in an infinite succession of moments which we call time, and outer perceptions must be located in a space which is infinite in extent. So we can know something only as it is seen in temporal succession or in a spatial location. Whatever might be other than or behind such natural events – that is, whatever might not be in time and space – we are simply unable to perceive and hence not gifted ever to know.

"I do hope you find I am making sense. I think I catch

a spark of interest in René's and Friedrich's eyes. I hope so. And Chang and Nagaraj, I'm delighted to note, don't seem as puzzled as David and Ludwig. I hope they will consent to speak up before the afternoon is over. I now accept this Copernician revolution as an unshakeable, because reasoned, basis for all my thinking. When I am by myself I distinguish between the objects of nature as we know them, that is, as they can be understood by human faculties – these I call appearances or phenomena, the objects of the everyday and of science – and the way things might be apart from the special limitations of human perceptions and human ways of thinking. Consider what we know about ourselves, for example. We see and touch our bodies in space and we perceive our feelings and inclinations as events in our inner sense of them. But this is not our true self, our soul, as we say; it is merely the appearance of our self in space and time. The true self inhabits a spaceless and timeless realm withdrawn from human knowledge. This I call the self as it is in itself.

"You can see now how I find I must disagree with the great Aristos and bother René. Human reason does not reach into the sphere where things are their true selves, where, as I believe, God and humans as spiritual beings reside. I hope this eliminates all future squabbling among metaphysicians. Our cognitive faculties are simply not effective in metaphysical questions, so there is nothing to squabble about. One further consequence of my distinguishing between appearances and things as they are in themselves is that reason, the very queen and goddess of human striving, can no longer be accepted as the faculty of scientific cognition. Here again I deviate from the views of our father and René. Reason demands total knowledge, absolute certainty of explanation, but the sciences never achieve this. Our ability to explain events always leaves some unknown factors even while allowing us to predict their occurrence. Reason is not responsible for scientific knowledge, though its demand for total cognition is the spur and condition of scientific investigation. It is another faculty – one which for my own purposes I call the understanding – that achieves whatever knowledge humans are capable of inside and outside of science.

"Reason – ah, that most powerful and beautiful of all words! – though not capable of cognition, has two functions of even greater importance. René is quite right, I believe, in holding that the idea of God, of a first, uncaused cause is innate in human reason. I would add that René's ego, the 'I', the individual soul, is an idea equally innate; and the idea of a perfected, self-contained cosmos, because it is self-evidently not derived from experience, belongs in the same class as well. These three ideas, innate in reason and given to our thinking by her, are not, however, objects which we can come to know. They appear to be, they deceive us if you like, they lure us into cognitive squabbles, but they lie outside the grasp of the understanding, our only cognitive faculty.

"But they are not useless. They hold before us the ideal of a perfect knowledge and so spur our theoretical endeavours even while they retire coquettishly before have tried to show, quite simple. An object that can be known must be able to appear within the concepts and the space and time of human experience. Do any of us really believe that God, the soul and the entire cosmos are going to turn up within the individual experience of any one of us and be perceivable in time and space? If we do we must either be lunatic or consider ourselves godlike.

"I can see I am trying your patience. Friedrich can hardly hold himself back and, if I'm not wrong, even Nagaraj looks as though he has thoughts on these matters. Well, perhaps you'll indulge an older brother just a little further, for I still have to tell you what final conclusion my thinking has brought me to. So far I have only set the stage for the main drama.

"Reason is not cognitive, not epistemic, I have said. Yet it is the highest human faculty. If anything can secure man's spiritual nature, his being beyond the perceived natural order, at least in part, it must be reason. But I have argued at length that it is not by its delusive claims to suprasensible *knowledge*, that reason can do this. You'll be wondering then, as I wondered for many years, how it can. What way is left? Here begins the main drama.

"It is in its *practical* employment, in the determination of the meaning and destiny of human life, in its *vivial* function, if you will permit a neologism, that reason comes into its own. It is through the problems of morals that metaphysical questions are dealt with. Now that must seem to you virtually nonsensical, and I see even the patient Nagaraj shaking his head.

"Let me remind you of a common and simple experience, what most of us would call, I think, our sense of duty. Everyone is familiar with the usually troublesome way in which, in the midst of our pleasantest inclinations, a sense of what we *ought* to do opposes our inclinations and, as it were, spoils the fun. Bear in mind that inclinations are aroused by affairs in the outside world and are directed back there for their fulfilment, that is, that they are a *passive* response to things in the sensible world; and bear in mind as well that the sense of ought is *active*, that is, does not arise as a response to an external stimulus; and that it is not directed at any objects in the natural world for its satisfaction. We can then see the beginning of a solution to my, or should I say, our problem. The ought, *das Sollen* as I say in my meditations, is spontaneous, self-generated. As it arises in opposition to our natural desires and hence is not part of them, it tells us unmistakably that it has another origin, that it comes from another realm; and that realm I call the suprasensible or intelligible realm. This spontaneity, this uncaused character of the *Sollen*, the moral ought, is, I firmly believe, given to our inner awareness immediately, without further need to discover it or prove its existence. It is a *factum*.

"Now I think very important conclusions hang on this *factum*. Spontaneity is by definition uncaused; it is self-evidently free of determination by all natural causes; it is not just the evidence for, but is itself the expression of, human freedom. The sense of ought intervenes as an expression of our own will; that means that it can be thought of as a will that is uncaused, or free. Further, ought is an imperative, not a mere suggestion; its authority is absolute; it is a kind of law for us. What ought to be, ought to be done for its own sake, unrelated to personal reward or punishment. So the ought is not only an unconditional imperative, but also a universal one; and these are the two marks of reason: necessity and universality. If you follow me in this you will understand how I can say that the moral imperative is the voice of reason. It is not reason in its theoretical use, of course; but it is reason in its practical or vivial employment. Freedom – and my entire course of thought turns on that one simple term – is a necessary assumption of reason in a being who believes himself to be conscious of a will that is other than the faculty of desire.

"The consequences of freedom for man's beliefs about the truths of God, soul and immortality are of course the fruit of all my inner wrestlings these many years. I have talked for such a long time already that I should stop now, and I would like to, but I owe you a few final words. It is clear to me that if man is free, then he is a spiritual being whose home is in the suprasensible or intelligible world, not the natural world which science studies. If his freedom means that he is pursuing moral perfection, as it does, and if this is an unending task, as it is, it follows that man must be immortal. All this is conceivable, however, only in a moral universe where worthiness is in harmony with happiness; and such a universe cannot be, obviously is not, guaranteed by the same laws of nature which circulate the blood through my body or sustain the planets in motion. But a moral universe is a demand of our reason and so must be secured by an omniscient and omnipotent divine being. For vivial purposes of the moral and religious life I assure myself in this way of the existence of God and the immortality of the human soul.

"Now a last word. Please note that I have made not one statement about the uses of reason that could be a contribution to metaphysics. I do not mean to add anything to our *knowledge* of these ultimate matters. I hope you will accept my belief that knowledge is a concept which is rootless and fruitless if we attempt to use it outside the sphere of the sciences and the everyday world. Nevertheless reason in practice assures us that for moral and religious purposes God is real; so are humans as spiritual beings and so is their immortality. We may be confident *that* God and ourselves as spiritual beings exist, but it would be illegitimate to employ any of the concepts and predicates of everyday and scientific knowledge to say *what* God and ourselves are. I have nothing but respect for our father and our younger brother René, but you can see how great are our differences. Unlike them I find no grounds for believing that reason is capable of knowing all things, including our deeply hidden selves and the remote and mysterious God.

"I agree with René, as I just said, that each of us can know *that* we exist, but I cannot agree that we can know *what* we are, for this would be metaphysical knowledge, is not vouchsafed us. René believed that through introspection he could encounter himself in the act of thinking, and so know himself as a thinking being. I believe firmly that such description holds only for the self as it appears to us in the inner events of our minds, but not as it is in itself, in its freedom beyond appearances, which is never given to us in any experience. And so you see how much my understanding of human life differs from René's. If we entrust our highest beliefs to the palsied embrace of metaphysics we shall lose them. They are secure only outside the realm of knowledge, argument and proof.

"But now I am overcome with embarrassment at having so immodestly taken up a large part of this lovely afternoon. Please forgive. Perhaps the shade of this benevolent old tree will temper our discussions."

Immanuel blew his nose callisthenically, took a sip from his glass of apple wine, and eased his legs for better listening. During the moments of awed silence that followed, the finer branches of the maple trembled briefly in a passing breeze and Friedrich, looking past Immanuel, thought he saw a cloud gathering on the horizon.

David

David naturally spoke next. Putting down the volume of Newton he had been leafing through, he took a pinch from his Parisian snuff box and said in his soft burr, "Oh brothers René and Immanuel, I fear you have been too long at your studies on the continent. You are still within the gnoseal influence of father Aristos, and yet you both betray him essentially. René agrees that knowledge is of divine inspiration, but he distinguishes truth from falsehood by a subjective certainty. This opens the door to scepticism. Immanuel uses the vocabulary of Aristos – 'reason' and 'knowledge' – but he breaks with him in substance. Reason no longer knows and knowledge fails to grasp the true nature of things. He opens the door even wider than René did to a creeping scepticism. What remains of reason, if it does not reason? You are both too unaware of the other sides and faculties of human nature – our feelings, our appetites, our passions. These are primary in founding an empirical science of man. It is time we put empty speculation behind us.

"I believe we should begin with what is most indubitably given us, namely the vast range of the immediate impressions that strike upon our minds, or souls, if you prefer that term. I mean all the perceptions coming from without which tell of an external world of bodies and events; and all our sensations, feelings and passions as they first appear in the mind. These impressions must be our touchstone, for they must of necessity appear to us in every particular just as they really are. Science and speculative reasoning have no source of knowledge other than our immediate impressions, which they merely combine or dissect theoretically.

"Ideas, memories and notions of the mind are but paled versions of the forceful, original impressions. That is why I can make no sense out of the inner nature of things as our father has always done, nor of Immanuel's shadowy things in themselves. Granted that we can never explain how external objects are related to our impressions of them – a red apple is red only for a sense organ that registers red perceptions, and yet we are incapable of imagining an apple without colour – we have no licence willfully to imagine a real world of things in themselves behind the world which our senses discover for us every day. Humans possess no faculty, whether Immanuel calls it understanding or René reason, which can, from its own sources, derive ideas that have worth as knowledge. Ideas are no more than faded copies of earlier impressions. That seems to me to put an end to idle reasoning about god or immortality or whatever else continental speculation entertains itself with. It is really quite simple: if I claim to *know* God or myself or the inner nature of a thing or a universal moral law, I must be able to show on which primary perceptions or sensations my knowledge of these reputed things is based. Where I am unable to do this, I must cease to make any claim that I *know* them – however much I *live* by them.

"You can see that I am not wholly out of sympathy with Immanuel's critical thinking on this point. We part company though when he derives the categories of scientific knowledge – reality, cause and effect, substance and attribute, and all the rest of his ingenious list – from the deep recesses of the mind, and allows them a mysterious cognitive function. If he and his continental teachers had observed the processes of knowledge more closely and speculated about them less I believe they would have noticed that all our categories of everyday, as well as of scientific, knowledge are nothing more than millennially entrenched habits of the mind. They are effective, that is, they evoke appropriate action in us and bind us carefully to things in the world, and so we believe them. Belief is an act of our feelings, not of our thinking nature and so our ideas cannot claim to yield knowledge in Immanuel's sense. They serve to accommodate us to the world according to our interests and needs, but they can do no more than anticipate the probable course of events; they cannot give us certain knowledge of them.

"Now the key to our ability to explain or to know or to predict is the relationship between events which we call causality. If we could know a cause and its effect, we would have certain knowledge of the way events are related. But a little observation of the way our minds work will put it beyond doubt that we do not and cannot ever come to *know* a cause. The reason for this I suggested a minute ago. It is that we never have a perception of any one event as a cause, as in and by itself *causing* another event. No more do we ever perceive an event as an effect, as being caused. Think of the way one croquet ball propells another. A direct perception of the efficacy which makes propulsion necessary is never vouchsafed us. We perceive only the movement of the first ball after being struck, its impact on the stationary ball and the commencement of motion in it. Thanks to our imagination and the force of habit we associate the first perception with the following ones and so come to believe that their connection not only is necessary in itself, but also tells us of a necessary connection, causality, between two events in the external world. I hope I have made it clear that our experience can never yield *knowledge* of such a relationship in the world of nature.

"Once we grasp this simple point there is an end to speculation about the limits of science and the province of pure reason. The problem need not and should not arise. There is no legitimate field of pure reason in philosophy, but only, in a certain sense, in mathematics. René and Immanuel and I must talk about this many times yet. Reason, in my view, is nothing more than the manipulation of distinct mental entities which we call ideas or notions. As these are but recollections, pale versions of distinct original impressions given in immediate experience, it follows that any rules for the manipulation of ideas must be applicable to the original experiences from which they derive. Ergo, reason has no freedom or authority to disgorge knowledge out of itself, as René believes it has.

"It follows from this that the majestic ideas of continental metaphysics – god, self, immortality, the very ideas that have entrapped Immanuel and René – are not to be established by argument of reason. Immanuel sees this up to a point, but even he attributes a quite unwarranted status to these ideas. I think debate on these questions need not be drawn out any further. We must learn to see the problems in a different way, free of moral and religious assumptions. Times are changing. We are justified less and less in holding to the classical faith in knowledge of the external world. In our day the task of philosophy should become the study of human nature. True, this is a kind of science, but it is empirical, not deductive. Let me illustrate.

"Look again at the problem of the personal self. What kind of an idea is this and where does it come from? A personal self must be single and enduring if it is to be worthy of its name, but if one searches for such a self among the jumbled contents of the mind it is not to be found. Our impressions are, without exception, fragmented and momentary. It follows that we cannot have an impression of a single, enduring, unchanging self, for, to speak in René's words, though quite contrary to his interest, no ego as a thinking substance is given to us in immediate awareness. Therefore there can be no knowledge of such. And when Immanuel believes that though we cannot know *what* our self is, we may be certain *that* it is, I would reply to him in the same way: which immediate inner impression do you point to when you entertain the idea of a suprasensible self? As we will readily agree that he can name no such impression, he should forthwith abandon the idea, though it is to too much to expect that he will.

"I would say the same about Immanuel's great discovery, the moral law. It is true that we have, some more often than others, an inner impression of a moral ought; but such an impression is just as fleeting and just as much compounded of pleasure and pain as any other of our inner impressions. To claim that it is a self-evident pronouncement of reason, even though subdued to its practical mode, is to confuse mythology with observation. It is, however, an important impression and it is this importance which arouses the imagination and actuates our capacity for forming mental habits and beliefs. Immanuel's moral law, which he hoped would ground human life in the suprasensible realm, is, analyzed empirically, just as much the deceptive product of some inner impressions worked over by imagination and habit as all other such lofty notions are. It cannot qualify as a certainty, even of *practical* reason."

David glanced around the circle of sceptical faces and went on. "I think I see a pyrrhonic smile of approval on the face of our oldest brother and I am happy that he should find something to approve of in my thinking. But I do not hold myself to be a sceptic of his fanatical persuasion. He urges us to withhold judgement in every case of perception and presumed knowledge because we cannot be certain what is true and what is false. What delightful irony! I see this as a dogmatic extension of the presumed sovereignty of reasoning, the very belief he wants to destroy. So I must disclaim it for myself.

"Reasoning, pursued singlemindedly, inevitably lures us into thickets from which there is no way out. In practice no one withholds judgement in every case; nature permits no such neutrality. We function as humans only *as* we judge what is true and what is false and what to do about it. Our capacity to hold the world together in a network of beliefs – in a personal self, in substantial things, in causality – takes the place of and indeed most usually assumes the appearance of knowledge. On this network of beliefs we base our judgements and by it we live. Dogmatic scepticism is as sterile and self-defeating as any other dogmatism, because it inflates the power and authority of reason and overlooks the governing function of natural belief in human life. It makes no sense to try to use the arguments of reason to invalidate the authority of reason. On his own principles the sceptic must first destroy reason, and that he cannot do. My defence against him is to ignore him. Pyrrhonic scepticism is not for me; I am persuaded that the need of our time is for a new science of man."

Friedrich

David finished and, flicking some stray snuff from his elegant waistcoat, inclined his head around the circle and lay back complacently on his elbows. There was no way of preventing the son of the fierce maenad from speaking next. Friedrich had been growing increasingly impatient as David spoke and now he was on his feet, loosing his dionysian energies into a flow of words he could not hold back.

"All respect to our aged father," he began, "who was great in his day and who has set the horizons to our thinking these many years. But our time is not his time, and our time demands a fresh beginning. The ancient philosophies have atrophied into barren philosophies of science; all our 'ologies are just so many dry stream beds twisting purposelessly through infertile wasteland. And it is we, my brothers, our family of philosophers, who are responsible for this degeneration. Since the time of the ancients we have venerated reason as the highest, the most god-like faculty in humans, and have singled out the problem of knowledge as the heart of the human predicament.

"That is a denigration, and in it lie the seeds of our

own confusion. Man is not primarily cognitive; he is in every cell and pulse of his being creative. Through him the creative power that is in all things expresses itself; by placing himself at the disposal of this power and so creating with it, man becomes everything he can be: his highest, his super self. Our 'philosophy', to use that dessicated word, our 'thought-work' I should say, or perhaps our 'thought-play', must, in this time of fresh beginnings, learn to see man in his fullness, and to see his faculty of reason and his pride of knowledge taking their subordinate place in that fullness. Henceforth our thinking should be devoted to furthering man's creative life, not to stifling it in swathings of spurious metaphysical theories.

"I agree with the adjuration of our aging father, that we must evoke the best genius of our time if we are to have a future humans can be proud of. We are balancing on a razor's edge. But it is not science, not even at its best, that can move us into the future. It is the fresh unleashing of forgotten life forces that is the great need. The society of the future Aristos envisaged will be founded not on a complex of his favoured sciences, but on a new morality, on a new acceptance of life, on a fresh complex of life-loving values, on a new humanity.

"You will understand from this that I cannot believe the views of René, Immanuel and David are any more likely to see us through the crisis in human history which is gathering around us. René believes that his cogitations are his true self, that he is, in substance, a cogitator and that his cogitations will secure us our life-truths. His body, I gather, is not part of himself. He suppresses it, the very seat and guardian of his life forces – his instincts, his passions, his dreams, even his philosophical fervour – below the level of philosophical relevance. And Immanuel's obsession with the cognition of our world, as though that were our primary relationship to things, is in the same tradition. Where are our living bodies? They cannot be suppressed and banished as citizens of a mechanical nature; they are our access to the creative forces. Immanuel's pallid 'inclinations' and 'desires' are a poor substitute for the driving force of our creative instincts. Even David, who spoke of the importance of feeling and imagination in human life, and who attacks the traditional claims of reason, is still a reasoner. He appears sceptical but remains safely within the gnoseal tradition of Aristos. He aims at a new *science*, not a new concept, of man. He and René and Immanuel are, each in his own way, generating confusion, I think. Each of them claims to break with the classical worship of knowledge and reason and to have found a new foundation for philosophy. But their thinking is at odds with their words. Each attempts to choke off incipient scepticism even while opening the floodgates of doubt into the hallowed fields of philosophy. I say we are confused and I hope they will forgive my bluntness."

Friedrich paused to catch his breath. His uncomfortably intense gaze met the more than a little abashed and dubious expressions of the others. René and Immanuel and David seemed to be thinking derogatory thoughts to themselves. Only the eldest brother and the two foster brothers betrayed a fascination with Friedrich's opening attack.

"How to begin a beginning, there's the problem," he went on. "I urge on everyone of us the need to exercise a ruthless scepsis toward every dogma, belief, law, opinion, value, that tradition cocoons us in. There is where we begin. René tried to do this and so did Immanuel and David. But they all stopped far short of the depth that scepsis demands. Scepsis must begin with what is nearest to us and most sacrosanct: our subtlest feelings and perceptions, the flow of life itself. Have you not noticed that there is a treacherous principle at work in the heart of even the simplest things? Doesn't the pervasive erring of things, their deceptiveness, their falseness, debilitate your naive trust, make you draw back from all that naively offers itself as true and self-evident? I begin by telling myself that the deceptive character of the world in which we believe we live is the most certain thing our understanding can fasten on – and I accept the paradox of that view.

"Don't we commonly assume that what we are aware of as passing through our minds, the contents of consciousness as we usually say – ideas, feelings, memories, and so on – are *all* we have in mind? It seemed to me that our older brothers, and surely our father as well, believe this. But where do the clear, precisely named contents of consciousness come from? They are not born the instant they emerge into the light of the awareness which assigns them names – 'fear', 'pain', 'good', 'bad', and so on. Follow them back, as I have tried to do, into the dim depths which lie under the lighted surface of our minds, and you will be frightened, as I have been, at the discoveries to be made there. Believe me, I have found good and evil so intertwined beneath the surface that my moral sense becomes a hindrance to my understanding. I find that the socially approved motives which I assign to my actions often have roots in my sub-mental regions which are their opposite, something I would be ashamed of. I even believe that the motive I approve of is often a form of deception on the part of its root or source. In order to perpetrate some evil deed I have to conceal its real character from myself by dressing up an acceptable motive for it.

"If you can accept this possibility, and I realize it is very new to you, imagine this twist, this falsification, which, I have discovered, takes place at the entrance to our everyday minds, being true for *all* matters of our awareness. Not only our moral judgements become false, but our intellectual judgements, our sense of truth, as well. Take that seriously and you will be able to see what I mean by the need for a ruthless scepsis. More than our father's philosophy ever dreamed of, our emotional, spiritual and intellectual lives are rooted in, even to a very great extent are captive to the turbulent world of the unconscious mind. Philosophers talk of the conscious mind as though it were sovereign, the divine element in us; but my thinking has led me to the view that our bodies, which are the seedbed of our inheritance and the seat of our motives and value judgements, are more important than our minds. 'Body' does not mean bones and flesh of course; it means the way creative life-forces becomes actual for us. When I say 'body' I am saying 'earth'. We will never know ourselves, or our potential, until we have learned to love the earth. Oh there is heaven too, but if that is all we can make real we will be swept away into the outer space of obsessive superstitions. We have no right to give the lie to our bodies. Our survival as a worthy species turns on our recovering a sense of the way life flows in all living beings. If we fail, our distorted minds will, once again, craft some comfortable habitat of false beliefs for humans to live in.

"Sometimes I think I am reversing the traditional world view, audacious as that sounds. Our tradition finds the world of the senses and the feelings the seat of error and delusion; the world of immaculate concepts, the kingdom of reason and knowledge, is the home of truth, where error is righted. In my thinking this isn't so. I find the work of reason is more likely to be of shoddy craftsmanship, rickety from unconscious misconceptions and dishonest motives. What my body, and remember that means my sense of life, allows me to experience *before* reasoning sets in – this I call my 'great' reason – is the seat of what wisdom I have. It is wiser than the little reason of the philosopher.

"Because I reverse the order of heaven and earth I can see a future for the human species that no one has yet dreamed of. We can become honest if we want to; we can acknowledge that the roots of our lives are neither good nor bad; we can accept them, whatever they are, just as they are in a kind of pagan reverence, because that will be ourselves. We can say 'yes' to everything that erupts within us and so allow it to be in its innocence. This is quickly said, but hardly done. It means we would need the courage to live with change, not stability, to be at home in the flow of life, not in the security of fixed ideas. After some years of brooding on this – all the years you thought I was studying ancient languages – I can say this afternoon for the first time, and I draw a deep breath before I say it, that *a new era in human history is possible if we follow my vision*. Men will no longer need to find their heaven remote from the earth and their eternity apart from time; they will find heaven *in* the innocent life of the earth and eternity *in* the unstaunchable flow of time. Those who can find the courage for this will become, as I put it, 'trans-human'."

Friedrich paused again and looked defiantly around the circle at the faces of his brothers. Immanuel cleared his throat as though he would interrupt, but then gestured his resignation; René and David remained silent in a mixture of disbelief and embarrassment; Ludwig shook his head in grim amusement; the brother from Elis regarded Friedrich with wondering approval; Chang and Nagaraj leaned forward in expressionless absorption.

Friedrich went on.

"All of us, perhaps excepting Ludwig, have been brought up to believe that philosophy proceeds by the ethereal movements of reason; that reason has its own innate laws; that properly exercised, it yields knowledge; that this knowledge is the highest truth of the unchanging, eternal way of things, of 'being' as the professors like to say. Oh my brothers, what a steaming jungle of fetish worship this tradition is. We must ask, it is the imperative of our time to ask, on what assumptions the movements of philosophic reason rest. I have in my solitude asked this question and the answer that has come to me is this: the life-germ of every philosophy is not in its reasonings but in its unconscious moral – or immoral – purposes. A philosophy expresses the life-sense, the life-drive of the philosopher. Philosophy does not uncover the structure of the world, it *forms* the world; it *is* the tyrannical imperative to form a world. Philosophy first forms a world and then reason discovers this same world as if it existed in its own right.

"I wonder and wonder at this and wonder how it could have happened. And I tell myself that it must derive from the underlying life-disposition of philosophers. They distrust and fear their own bodies and senses and feelings because these are opaque and a threat to reason's sovereign clarity. They try desperately to grasp birth and life in dead concepts. They kill life as it comes to them, and stuff and embalm its members with their eternal ideas. Metaphysics is a macabre game played with mummified fragments of life. With all brotherly affection I find René's clear ideas of 'thinking', 'doubting', 'self', 'god', and 'reason as the light of nature' beautiful and delusive instances of just this activity. Immanuel's splendid table of scientific categories is an even more striking instance of the retreat from the fearsome and lovable chaos of life to the tombs of the philosopher's mummies. Even his 'ideas of reason' – god, the immortal self and so on, the foundation of our moral and religious life – are not truths of 'practical reason'. Such ideas, I very much fear, and I can see Immanuel's annoyance with me growing, are but the luxuriant weeds of the confused presumptions in which reason necessarily entangles itself.

"I simply must go one step further, and I am happy our father has seen fit to leave us to our own thoughts this afternoon, because I have decided that his famous eternal truth of reason, his statement of the very nature of reason – that one and the same thing cannot be said to be and not to be at the same time, the law of non-contradiction – must be unseated from its throne. The law of non-contradiction is not a necessary truth about things, but rather a discovery of our own incapacity. *We* are incapable of affirming and denying one and the same thing. But as the sense world comes to us only in contradictory ways – birth is dying, what is seen is seen as touchable, what is heard is heard as shape, and so on – it seems to me that the law of non-contradiction hardly reflects the order of nature. Aristos' law of thought is rather a subjective necessity, or perhaps a practical rule; in any case it is empirical. However, as our practical uses of reason depend on it, I agree that it can be accepted as a means toward our survival.

"There is a further ground for repudiating a law of human reason as an absolute truth about things. In order to be sure the law holds for *things*, we would have to know from some other source that in the realm of real things contradictory attributes do not inhere in the one thing. Now, as we have no such knowledge, it must follow that our father's famous 'law' tells us that we *should* not think contradictories, that is, that a human world is better constructed without them. In short, a rule of reason is not a truth about things; it is an observation about human limitations.

"Now please, don't rise up against me yet, for there is more to come. You might think that even if reason is not a faculty that yields us knowledge, there might be other faculties that do – the understanding, science, commonsense, and so on. But I believe it is not so. *There is no faculty of knowledge vouchsafed to humans*. In spite of popular belief – I might say popular superstition – the newer experimental sciences do not yield what we traditionally understand as knowledge. Why? Well, simply because the idea of knowledge is unintelligible; we have no way of making the idea of knowledge conceivable, that is, conceivable as possible for us. Knowledge doesn't take place. It was arrogance for us to dream of it. We are not heavenly beings; we are heavy with the richness of earth. Our world is pure becoming, and the nature of becoming cannot be formulated; it is false, self-contradictory, unintelligible. My brothers, hear me well: I say becoming – remember human life is nothing else – and knowledge exclude each other."

Friedrich paused, a gleam of triumph in his eye, and brushed his moustaches hastily. "We misconceive knowledge and why we need it. What we habitually call knowledge is more a kind of ordering, of schematizing, or imposing on the chaos of life as much form and regularity as our will to live and to create must have. The will to knowledge – I could equally well say the will to truth – is the will to make a durable, secure habitat for the species. It is the will to transform the 'false' character of the world as it initially comes to us into something unchanging, something that will merit the name 'being'. In short, the will to truth is the will to *make* true. Truth does not exist before the will; it is something created. Truth is the name for a process, a process of mastery over our unruly environment, a process which has only itself as its purpose. The will to truth is the will to power, it is the creative urge to unfold the grandest potential of humans. What we call knowledge functions as a means to this end. Can you understand me now if I say that as everything we deem knowledge is in truth error, truth is simply that kind of error without which our species could not survive. We are told of an ancient thinker, more ancient even than our father, who said to an astounded world, 'We cannot *think* what does not exist.' And today I say the opposite: 'What *can* be thought must certainly be a fiction.'

"I see that I shock you. But I cannot regret it or do otherwise. We must all learn to think in radically new ways. David's attack on reason was encouraging, but he stopped short, his scepsis failed him. His many 'beliefs', in which we live and which take the place of Immanuel's categories of knowledge, are not self-explanatory. If he looks more deeply into their roots he will discover that they are not innocent substitutes for knowledge but express our will to survive, and lie outside any form of truth. As for Immanuel's distinction between the concepts of science, which guarantee us knowledge of the world, and the ideas of morals and religion which, he holds, have merely a practical usefulness for life, I would like to say to him: Why make this distinction? If you could see that scientific categories function essentially in the same way as your moral and religious ideas do, that is as constructive hypotheses on which we can base further exploration, on which we must *dare* to live, then you and I would be very close to agreement.

"As for Immanuel's moral law, I must admit that it is too much for me. That I have a strong sense of duty from time to time is clear. But to place names on that sense is surely difficult and treacherous. Observation of inner events is as fraught with error as outer perception is. For my part, I hear no voice of *reason* speaking to me through the stirring of my conscience. If anything, it will be the voice of a profound discontent. René's observations of himself 'thinking' are open to the same basic objection. I find I can directly *observe* very little of what he reports. He is, as I think, a victim of our language. Just because the verb 'think' requires a subject, we unthinkingly suppose that the *process* referred to by the word 'thinking' must itself have a substantive subject, a doer, *someone who* is the thinker. And René supposes that this thinker must be what the word 'I' refers to, a necessity which is not at all evident. The 'I' is itself just one of the chaotic phenomena observed in introspection and has no credentials as the hidden subject of thinking. In brief, a painful, unbrotherly brief, I find René's foundation of reasoning a shambles of faulty expectations, faulty observations and faulty understanding of language. I hope he will forgive my ruthless words.

"I think I have made my point and it is time for me to sit down. I have a last thought though. Immanuel's Copernican revolution is a stroke of great promise, but it doesn't go far enough. As I said, it appears to secure scientific knowledge and to justify religious belief at one stroke. In effect though, it opens the door to profound scepticism without realizing it, and so confuses hopelessly. What if we attempted a language revolution? All our philosophies rest on a hidden faith in the objective validity of our languages. We have always assumed that some simple existent, some reality, corresponds to the names we use in speaking. We assume that the words 'being', 'knowledge', 'moral law', 'cause', 'effect', 'mind', 'will', 'self', 'god', are names for things that have waited patiently through the aeons to be discovered by us and have their labels pasted on them. And this most basic of all philosophical assumptions has not one sound argument to support it. Philosophical terms, far from embodying our wisdom, spring up at precisely the key points of our ignorance; they are fictions, and usable only as such, consciously. To acknowledge this and draw the consequences is the revolution I speak of. Hitherto we have believed that our languages conform to and tell us about the structure of the world. We believe it is because things have qualities, for example, and because in every action some agent is acting, that our languages are made up of noun words and adjective words, of verbs and their subjects, and so on.

"How would it be if we reversed this relationship? How would it be if we assume that the world of things conforms to and reflects the grammar of our languages? Think of the freedom that gives our imagination, our thinking and our living. We would no longer need to be trapped by linguistic habit into believing that creation must have a creator – I've often thought that we will believe in god as long as we believe our languages reflect realities – that thinking must have a thinker and willing a self who wills. The majestic panorama of the universe is opened to our free exploration and creative re-making. This would be the revolution to complete Immanuel's. This would free humans to become more than humans have ever known how or dared to be. This would free humans to accept gladly as their own destiny the unnameable creative forces surging through them. This would free humans to find their eternity in the endlessly inexhaustible ebb and flow and recurrence of all things great and small. This would free humans to overcome themselves, so to speak.

"And, my brothers, it would free us all from the enthralment of ancient philosophies; we would no longer need them for our truth. New modes of thinking would emerge for our rescue.

"Oh I know, these are but ideas, nearly empty, but the future grandeur of the species, indeed – and hear me well – the *survival* of the human species turns on our ability to think and live out their furthest consequences.

"Now I sit down. You are annoyed that I have usurped so much of this lovely afternoon, but you are also patient in your impatience. Please forgive; but more important, heed what I have told you."

And Friedrich sat down against his stone, breathing deeply to ease the heavy flush in his face and wiping the moisture of his excitement from his moustaches.

The east wind had been freshening while he spoke and as he sat down the top of the maple swayed suddenly and the thickening clouds low in the sky infused a silent unease through the tiny circle.

Ludwig

For a minute no one moved; all were numbed by Friedrich's vehemence. And then Ludwig, who had been sketching building blocks and showing little interest in the talk of his brothers until Friedrich spoke of the importance of language, buttoned his velvet jacket purposefully and, still seated, began to speak. "Excuse my bluntness, brothers," he said, "but I cannot make sense of all this talk, excepting only of what Friedrich said about language. What makes you think there can be any truth or falsehood in arguments about suprasensible realms, moral laws, immortal souls and all the rest? There is no way to resolve such arguments. Have you never asked yourselves why you cannot agree among yourselves? I have been asking myself just that these many years, and I think there is a very good reason.

"Quite bluntly, I have come to the conviction that philosophical problems are not *about* anything, even though the language you use to spin them out makes it appear as if they were. There *are* no philosophical problems as René and Immanuel understand them. René says reason yields knowledge of god's attributes, as though we could be sure in solid terms what the words 'reason', 'knowledge', 'god', are meant to do for us, that is, to what familiar language situations they lead us. René uses these terms in ways which do not, and cannot, connect up with the logic of their everyday use – that is, their natural, proper use. I could say he breaks the rules society has evolved over a long, long time for the usage of such words. The word 'reason', for example, belongs in a context of careful argument and objective proof, not of religion. 'Knowledge' belongs in a finespun context of confident behaviour, not of intuitive conviction. 'God' belongs in situations of worship and reverence, not in metaphysics.

"Immanuel, in his turn, disputes René's claims because these pivotal terms, in Immanuel's use, derive from and are designed to allow us to cope with different concrete experiences. Immanuel's 'reason' is the voice of our aspirations and of the highest moral law, but yields no knowledge. 'Knowledge' is a true description of everyday and scientific processes and objects. 'God' is not an object to be known but a postulate, a necessary truth following from the moral imperative in us. God is related to our behaviour, not our science.

"So the argument goes on. René and Immanuel will never agree because their argument is not like arguing whether the apples on the tree are ripe or not. In such cases we know how to follow the words in dispute back into shared situations which of themselves will decide the matter for us. Ripe means edible and to decide that you bite into the apple.

"But philosophical disputes are bootless. They merely hurl private soliloquies back and forth. René and Immanuel are expecting their words and their speech to do the impossible for them. They select some well-understood, everyday terms and project them upwards into a foreign, metaphysical realm. They assume they will retain their familiar behaviour and meanings in this unnatural habitat. But they don't and they can't. Quite simply, there are no accepted rules for the use of words like 'reason', 'knowledge', 'god', once they are removed from their age-old historical and social milieu. I cannot conceal my view that the philosophical talk of René and Immanuel is erudite and skilful nonsense.

"We will have to learn to see that language is not a *duplicate* of the world, a lexicon of meanings *about* the world, but is *part of* the world, as integral to human situations and endeavours as feelings, behaviour, natural forces and social conventions are. That is why language does not invoke a realm of meanings distinguishable from the world and from itself, but functions within social contexts to further the common work at hand. In this, its everyday and proper use, language has, or makes, sense. When we use everyday language for other than its proper purposes, however – and philosophical discourse is the clearest and most extreme example of this misuse – we begin to talk nonsense, that is, our talk no longer furthers a productive human enterprise.

"René's 'I think' is a perfect example. To say 'I think' as a way of marking off one's own opinion from the opinion of another, or to mark off 'thinking' from 'dreaming' or 'feeling', is sensible talk. In such cases we all know how to pick up the phrase 'I think', what value to put on it, how to react to it and what to expect next. It fits into an accepted logic of language. But when René lifts that phrase into the sky of his metaphysics and believes that it allows him to discover an eternal, spiritual self behind the word 'I' and to discover a pure, autonomous mental process, 'thinking' behind the word 'think', of which the 'I' would be the agent thinker, then he is no longer making sense. I would like to get him and Immanuel to see that their philosophical problems are no problems – except of course the problem of seeing that they aren't.

"We must at last, in our own great day of new beginnings, as Friedrich would say, realize this. Our interest, as the heirs to philosophy, must become to test the talk we hear around us, and especially the talk we hear from ourselves, for its sense and for its nonsense. To show a fellow philosopher that his problem arises from tearing language expressions out of everyday contexts, where they are at home and where they can be used with good sense, and then using them in his philosophical argument with the false expectation that they still make sense – to show that is all a philosopher can do. I hope we can all learn to see that traditional philosophy has been predominantly nonsense. Philosophers have been like flies trapped in a fly bottle of ignorance about language. The new way of thinking must show them the way out.

"I am sure of what I say, and yet there remains a paradox. I study the way language behaves, I point out its limitations and improper uses, but I am doing this by employing the very language I am analyzing. This must suggest to everyone that everyday language is capable of more than I say it is, for the analysis I undertake is not itself an everyday use of language. I sometimes wonder if I am caught up in the absurdities of which I accuse the rest of you. There is one conclusion though that I will stake my life on: language is surrounded by mystery, language is a mystery. Still, our light is to stay with what we can be sure of. And we can be sure how to test our talk for its good sense or its useless nonsense by forcing it back to everyday situations where it is at home. If I can get you to see that metaphysics is nonsense, even though to say that is itself nonsense, I will have done something."

Ludwig paused, as if undecided whether to say no more or to go on. He stretched his legs and was about to unbutton his jacket, when his face tightened, he crossed his legs again and leaned forward to speak.

"I should add something," be began. "I am afraid I have left language levitating in mid-air. It is not enough to say that our speech makes sense if we confine it to social situations within the accepted rules of everyday usage. I myself thought for a long time that that was as far as we need go. Of late, however, I have realized that speech is not a social activity grounded in its own logical rules. Speech does not simply accompany and further our practical, artistic, moral and religious behaviour while remaining grounded in its own logic and drawing its sense from within itself. My latest thinking leads me to view this as untrue. I must correct myself. The Ludwig that thought that way is now deceased. In a way, what I have decided I must now say is a kind of posthumous revelation, if you'll excuse my macabre humour.

"I can put my latest views in the form of three radical insights which I believe I will take with me to the grave. I am not oblivious to the way they conflict with what I have just said, nor do I apologize. My earlier and latest views each have their justification and I prefer to let them stand side by side. Much of what I want to add now is compatible with what Friedrich told us and perhaps with what David said as well.

"I have come to the conviction that all our human logic, that is to say, what makes sense in our speech, is without principles and does not have its ground in itself.

"I have come to the conviction that sense in speech is grounded in our actions, in ways of behaving, in ways of living.

"I have come to the conviction that what I can say in words derives its sense from a background of untouchable assumptions – our communal cultural origins – and ultimately from a non-speakable mystery. I would presume to tell you something about these new convictions of mine if you have the patience. You may blame my loss of taciturnity on the greatness of this arboreal afternoon.

"I will try to speak briefly. I can see now that, in the end, we cannot describe how the logic of language works. We can only become aware of it. The difficulty for me, and for most of us, will be to grasp that our basic beliefs, the assumptions that ground all our speech and thinking, are themselves groundless. We like to distinguish between self-evident principles and the personal judgements that follow from them. This separates 'truth' from subjective error. But I now see that our principles of logic, that is, of what lends sense to speech, are themselves just judgements which we make in the interests of establishing a coherent system. We like to think that we hold to a 'philosophy,' or a general conception of the world, as a result of reasoning our way carefully toward it, that is, because we have reason to think it is true. But I now believe that our picture of the world is much more the slowly accumulated, in large part inherited, background to our thinking. It is the basis on which I decide what is true and what is false. It is more the source of reason than the result of it.

"You will all see how far I am from thinking, as Immanuel does, that our religious and moral life is founded on the universal truths of practical reason. I have come to believe that religion and morals derive their authority from a correlative way of life which is far below the level of words and reasons.

"Our personal picture of the world seems to be made up of a cluster of beliefs or convictions which form a system. The beliefs are quite primitive. I believe, for example, that this body is *my* body, that these hands and feet are *my* hands and feet. I believe that the morning comes before the evening, that the world existed long before I saw it. I believe that our speech brings us into immediate touch with a world of real things. Now none of these beliefs can be proved true, yet, as a system, they provide the life element within which argument and proof can be sustained. They are not so much self-evident as they are a given set of assumptions which we are not free to vary arbitrarily. The use of language in any context is possible only if we begin by trusting a system of beliefs. In sum, the logic of language is without ground. It is neither rational nor irrational; it is simply there, even as our whole life is.

"I'm sure this must strike you as negative, even destructive. But my latest thinking hasn't stopped there. I've tried in two ways to find a new basis for understanding how language is ultimately grounded. For one, I began to see that action, behaviour, is both the issue and the anchor of our speech. For the other, I slowly became convinced of what I have suspected for a long time, namely, that human speech derives its ability to carry meaning from what is unspoken and perhaps is unspeakable. I would like to say a few words about each of these matters.

"It is obvious that words are themselves a kind of deed, a refinement of our primitive reactions. As the great poet said, 'In the beginning was the deed.' Now I would say more. Our speech gets its full sense only from the actions which accompany and follow it. If we trace a line of argument back to its first grounds, we do not find there, so I now believe, some self-evidently true propositions, something we intuitively grasp. It is nothing other than our actions which lie at the bottom of every language game. Indeed, I would say that the mark of certainty in argument is our willingness to act on the assumptions of that argument, and without having any doubts. If I say 'I know this is my hand and this is my foot,' that becomes the basis of my entire behaviour toward my body and its worth. I would even go so far as to say that certainty of knowledge expresses a tranquil confidence in the way of things. I like to regard this tranquil confidence as a way of life. When I'm talking to myself I call it a *Lebensform*.

"This close transition, from what I claim to know in words to the consequences of those words for my behaviour, is the mark of genuine certainty in thinking. We assume, for example, that our world did not pop into existence a few seconds ago but has been in existence for some time. Such elementary assumptions make up the foundation of all our speech. They are the basis of our behaviour and of our thinking. I have gone so far at times as to believe that what ultimately counts in our talk – our promises, our faiths, our truths –

are not the words which one pronounces out loud, nor even what one thinks as one talks, but what concrete, significant difference our words make to our lives at critical turning points. I would say to you bluntly, and ask you to ponder it: it is praxis, our behaviour, the life we lead, that gives our words their full sense.

"You have all – excepting, of course, Chang and Nagaraj – thought of me in the past as a kind of mechanical, rule-giving speech logician, and I have come to see that that is what I was. My latest work has forced a wider horizon of awareness on me and, at times, even a kind of humility. I now doubt if we can give positive justification for the results of our conceptual analyses. It seems more likely that all our inquiries are set up and proceed so as to exclude their essential assumptions from doubt. They lie apart from the route of the inquiry, are exempt from it, and yet are what makes its conclusions possible. The questions we pose for ourselves and the explicit doubts which shape their investigation are grounded in the fact that other basic propositions are exempt from doubt. These utterly unquestioned, dead-certain assumptions make inquiry possible. They form the hinges, so to speak, on which our questioning swings. If I tried to put *everything* into doubt as René did, I would confront pure nothingness, as it were. That some things cannot be doubted belongs to the essence of our use of language, our way of thinking. How this runs strongly counter to René's method of doubting everything is so plain that I need not dwell on it.

"The relationship between what I believe I know or *can* understand and the assumptions which I do *not* understand seems very close. I sometimes think that I believe I understand something only because I am blind to all that I do not understand, to the extent of my own ignorance. This is sobering. Could it be that what I cannot put into words – what seems mysterious – forms the background against which what I can say clearly acquires its meaning? I think the semitic strain in me may be coming to the surface. The gulf seems so great between the natural order of our speech and a supranatural order which would be quite beyond the reach of natural speech. Perhaps only the supranatural can give expression to the supranatural.

Before I lapse into silence allow me a personal observation about the course of our discussion thus far. It is as if history were being compressed into a few hours. Progressively, from René to Immanuel to David to Friedrich to myself, the faith in the sovereignty of knowledge – one might say the religion of philosophy – has, so it seems to me, eaten into itself, has eroded from within, thanks to its own endeavours. You have been attempting to buttress philosophy – we must except Friedrich – the while your thinking has been inexorably undermining it. Together we have not left much of Aristos' dream intact. Friedrich may have a truer sense of the future than any of us.

"And now my last word. You have all been very patient, allowing one who does nothing but criticize you to speak for such a long time. Is it true for all of you, as I have realized it is for me, that, however diligently one works at philosophy, the results are mere lifeless exhibits of a linguistic skill, lacking lasting worth, unless and until thinking is illumined by a light which comes from outside one's own self?"

Ludwig stopped in mid-thought, appeared to be embarrassed at the personal turn his remarks had taken, and closed his lips firmly. His eyes turned inward as he sat back, stretched out his legs and slowly unbuttoned his jacket.

The Brother From Elis

René and Immanuel restrained their impulse to defend themselves long enough for David to turn to the patient brother from Elis. "Revered brother, you have known our father's views longer than any of us and are his most radical critic. Your name is virtually synonomous with scepticism. Won't you tell us plainly what you think of his philosophy of knowledge and of our family disputes this afternoon?"

The oldest brother hesitated for a moment or two, nodded his round-cropped head and, as if reluctantly, spoke. "The master," he began, "is, as I think, engaged in a different enterprise than I am. He is working to *know*, that is, to seize the nature of all things through an accurate description of them, using concepts. In one degree or another each of you is engaged in the same enterprise, though Friedrich and Ludwig are trying with great courage to break free and are almost succeeding. René believes that the purpose of his thinking is to *know* himself as a spiritual being, to *know* god as omniscient and benevolent, to *know* the principles of the new sciences. Immanuel is more modest but still believes that, thanks to the inborn concepts of the mind, we can unerringly *know* the behaviour of objects in our world. David, though repudiating all objective causal knowledge, still accepts our beliefs and sense impressions and feelings as something we can name and *know*.

"Friedrich struggled valiantly to carry through a radical scepsis of all claims to knowledge, but in the end, and quite contrary to his own intent, he speaks of consciousness, of a principle of illusion, of creative forces and a new eternity, as though these were realities known to him with all the traditional certainty of cognition. Ludwig attempted to set aside the entire philosophic tradition with his emphasis on the givenness of our language behaviour. But to believe that we have access to language behaviour as a realm of fact or reality is surely to leap over the first of all philosophical questions. This belief reminds me of the empiricist presumption that sense perceptions are given to our minds in their naked reality and that they are the basis of all knowledge. Ludwig and the empiricist are positivists and, as I think, suffer from the same naiveté.

"Now I must add that Ludwig's 'posthumous' views, as he calls them, move some distance toward my own convictions. I am thinking in particular of his late insistence that what we call knowledge or truth is not grounded in reason, but is sustained by our readiness to stake our life fortunes on what we believe we know. I liked his insistence that the certainty of knowing derives from a tranquil confidence in the way the world must be. Of course, Ludwig's thinking still leaves us with a cleavage between thinking and behaving which must somehow be healed. And he treats thinking and knowing with a happy confidence that ignores the crippling effects of scepsis.

"However, speaking for myself, I find the human predicament is not resolved primarily through knowledge, but by taking certain decisions about the nature of human well-being. This is more a matter of a discipline of thought and of appropriate attitudes than it is of knowledge about things. Philosophical problems, even those of David and Friedrich and Ludwig, arise, have their purpose and run their course *within* the concern of human well-being, either furthering or hindering it. I do not believe philosophical problems have a life of their own which runs its course toward purely conceptual solutions.

"David was quite right when he said I urged the suspension of judgement. Having found that our simplest sense experiences do not permit us to determine the nature of *things* – the sweet taste of honey does not permit us to know that honey is sweet apart from our tasting – I have decided that we must withhold judgement, not claiming to know whether honey is sweet or not, or indeed whether it is both sweet and not sweet, or neither. If suspension of judgement, that is, a refusal to claim knowledge, becomes a steadfast attitude in all life situations – even where the judgement concerns what is good or bad and not merely what is sweet or not sweet – there ensues a serenity of mind which is the truest well-being that humans are capable of. I would say that the unaware telos, the natural fulfilment – not, if you please, the calculated reward – of suspending judgement is serenity of mind. Suspension of judgement, as a principle, is more than a theory about the impossibility of knowledge; it is a life attitude and so has implications for man's well-being. Knowledge by itself, even encyclopaedic knowledge, cannot lead to well-being. Knowledge, in itself, is indifferent to well-being. From this you can see that my undertaking differs from the master's, and, I think, from that of all of you, though in varying degrees. My views are ancient though they have perhaps never entirely disappeared. After listening to your earnest talk this afternoon I wonder if the day of radical scepsis is not upon us again.

"It will not be easy to expose the groundless claims of knowledge in an age of wonderful science. I tried and failed in my own day, many years ago. I never overcame the lure of the seemingly true givenness of experience, any more than René, David and Ludwig have been able to do. My scepticism is crippled by my inability to surrender the comfort of knowledge totally, and I realize this. During my sojourn in Nagaraj's homeland I learned much from the pundits but never grasped how they supplant knowing with behaviour. This afternoon Friedrich's great adventure ran aground on the same rocky shore.

"I do not hesitate to tell you plainly that for the new future men's thinking will hinge on this question: How can we make sense of total scepticism? Or, how can the human need to make sense out of life be fulfilled in the absence of the certainty which knowledge gives us?

"I think we are fortunate that our two foster brothers are with us this afternoon. Both are deeply learned in this question which has come to haunt us. May they speak up freely."

The Storm
Assault From Without

Chang

Ludwig looked quizzically at Friedrich, and Friedrich triumphantly at David, and David complacently at Immanuel, and Immanuel helplessly at René. In the deep silence the branches of the maple rustled to life in the strengthening wind. It was René, laying aside his beads, who spoke. "Something strange stirs in me, something exciting and uncomfortable," he said "when I listen to our brother from Elis. I have the eerie feeling that great ideas are brushing us with their wings. They are like faint memories that were once ours, yet they remain foreign and haunting. I don't think I have the heart to argue further just now."

Friedrich leaned into the circle from his rock and made a suggestion. "Our elder brother is a breath of fresh mountain air. I agree with his view that the primary concern of thought is not knowledge, though I can't accept his 'suspension of judgement' and 'untroubledness of soul' as adequate to the human predicament. It occurs to me that he was several years in the homeland of our new foster brother Nagaraj. Could it be that Nagaraj can throw more light on what he has just told us? Shouldn't we invite him to speak?"

The pause of decorum was marked but brief. Nagaraj appeared to awaken from a light meditation in time to acknowledge Friedrich's invitation. He adjusted his ochre robe over his left shoulder, raised both hands to his forehead in the eastern greeting, and spoke: "Much of what your elder brother says is strangely familiar and I remember stories about his countryman, the great Alexander, from my own childhood. But so much of what you all have been saying is alive in my own thinking – it is exhilarating to feel at home among such great thinkers – that I am afraid if I speak now I might run on tiresomely. May I suggest that my fellow foster brother from the land of the ancients, Chang, tell us first what he thinks of your great father's philosophy and of your sceptical criticisms, and then, if there is anything left to say and your patience is not in shreds, I could try to tell you how my tradition, the buddhist, has thought about some of your problems."

The silence which prevailed and the slight inclination of heads indicated agreement and the faces around the circle turned toward the other foster brother.

Chang settled his pointed black hat more firmly on his head, gathered his legs under him afresh and spoke in a small voice. "Good brothers," he said, "unlike Nagaraj I am not greatly exercised by your subtly refined problems, though I am fascinated by the zeal with which you attack them. One question puzzles me relentlessly as I listen to you all in the calm of this lovely summer afternoon. It is this. On what grounds do you believe that *argument* is so conclusive, or even so important, in establishing the truth of your philosophies? You have all put your minds deep into the sense of human life and the riddle of human destiny. Do you really believe that argument is your means of penetration and the ground on which your beliefs will rest? Do you really believe that argument has ever been more than a source of pride and a provocation to dispute?

"In my tradition we hold that the everyday world – where arguments arise, have their force, and end – is based on a naive acceptance of conventional words and names which are, as we say, merely the guests of reality, not its substance. The fine weave of everyday conventions is a front for men's private schemes, a front that masks their true intentions and houses the root errors of existence. Argument, the apotheosis of the magic of names, does not weaken trust in the superstitions of convention, but strengthens it. Argument, even philosophical argument, is the activity of what we call the 'little understanding'. This understanding fastens on the reality of our personal aversions and likings and so, entangling us in the 10,000 things, makes it impossible for us to see the harmony of heaven and earth, the oneness of all things.

"But there is a 'great understanding' and it functions differently. The great understanding makes no use of everyday categories and is free of personal entanglements. It takes things as in the oneness of the great *tao* which knows no boundaries and is outside the realm of fixed forms. This way of seeing we call clarity. It is, if I may be free with your revered language, a knowing that does not know. The great understanding rests in what it does not understand and that, we think, is the finest understanding. It is like listening to the stillness inside one where, if I may mix my words, light is born. Mind and knowledge, the little understanding, remain on the outside. Truth is not a point of view sustained by disputation, but is a way of seeing, or taking, things. If you ask me what is that way, I would answer, annoyingly perhaps, but I have no other way of saying it: the way of a true man. There must first be a true man before there can be truth. But the true man's truth is not knowledge; he doesn't *know* his truth. The true man rolls all things into the one *tao*, that is, he succeeds in living with all things so as to bring them together in one harmony, and . . ." Chang added with a smile, "without argument."

"Ludwig's last thoughts point to a breakdown of the wall that has held thinking and behaviour apart for so long, in your family. May it happen. I hope so. But even if it crumbles completely, what will you do without a radically different kind of discipline, what might be called a life-discipline, that could bind them together again?"

The gentle Chang looked around at his foster brothers and apologized. "Please forgive if I speak bluntly and appear not to appreciate your great labours. Perhaps I do not understand their purpose and the worth of your refined arguments."

Nagaraj

The brothers were silent. René looked intrigued, Immanuel quizzical, David interested, Ludwig dubious; Friedrich's eyes shone under his eyebrows. Nagaraj waited. "Is it enough?" he asked. The brother from Elis leaned forward to catch the attention of the others and shook his head emphatically. "No," he said, "It is not enough. Nagaraj can speak for the tradition, the Sanskrit, which is closest to our own philosophy; though I am sure he will not want his thinking called philosophy. Let us hear what he thinks of our master, and of our halting, familial attempts at scepsis. Put away your beads and engineering sketches, your comforting aphorisms and Newtonian ambitions. Let Nagaraj speak and let us listen. The challenge of Aristos is still ringing around our circle: scepticism tends to nihilism; if we abandon the life-enabling security of science we must be sure we have something mightier to put in its place. That was his warning.

"Thus far today we have slowly but irreversibly eroded his faith by our own philosophies and in spite of our intentions. Throughout this momentous devolution – from René's subjective rationality, to Immanuel's critical amputation of reason's functions, to Friedrich's dithyrambic embrace of life, to Ludwig's relentless dissolution of the last roots of logical reason – which will shape the spiritual topography of the times ahead, scepticism has reared up as a mountain range to be crossed. Yet no one of us has been able to make the crossing. We cannot do it within our own tradition. Even attacking Aristos is possible only by using some arrows from his quiver.

"But can we be sure that our tradition embraces every possible way of making sense out of human life and destiny – which is what our philosophies are for? In philosophical conscience let us hear from another classical culture how men have found good sense in life amid all the nonsense. Let Nagaraj speak out and let us listen, say I."

The natural sons of Aristos sat in silence after their revered elder brother had spoken. Puzzlement was in their faces, but also annoyance at the implied offence in his words. A second classical culture? A second tradition of philosophy independent of their own? How could philosophy be possible in default of the autonomy of the cognitive faculty and its laws of reason? Nothing but poetry or religious superstition could result, surely.

They turned their eyes back to the brown-skinned, bare-polled monk in his ochre robe sitting between the elder bother and Chang. And they saw that he had left the family circle and was deep in another world. In lotus position, eyes open, he was absent, and yet present in a real sense. His composure reached them all, dissolving petulance. The philosophic spirit of the brothers returned and they said to themselves, "Tolerance is the mother of learning. Could he possibly help us to cross the mountain range of scepticism?"

It was Immanuel who spoke for them all. "It is good, elder brother. Let Nagaraj speak and let us listen."

Overhead the maple suddenly lashed back and forth in a burst of wind, and black clouds, now close by, rumbled and growled. Under the tree the air became still as the brothers gathered their interest toward the meditating monk in his lotus posture.

Sensing this Nagaraj became present for them again and spoke, as if he had been inside their thoughts throughout. Raising his hands again in the anjali salute, he began. "How great of you to invite me, a stranger, to tell you what I think of your illustrious father and your own wrestlings to free yourselves from ancient dogmas. It was wonderful to hear Aristos pronouncing his deep faith in people, in science, in the human future. We too, we Sanskrit thinkers and buddhists, have a deep faith, but it is not in science or history or even in people as they are in the conventional world. Of all your father's ideas I was most struck by his faith in the ability of the human mind to penetrate the inner nature of things by means of knowledge. This leaves me deeply troubled. Immanuel and David were cautiously sceptical of this belief, I was happy to hear, but it was Friedrich who dared to say that all our everyday categories, no less than those of science or even than Immanuel's ideas of reason, are but human ways of overlaying a manageable order on the chaos of experience. I understand him to mean that they do not, as we commonly believe, yield knowledge, and our reasoning does not grasp the nature of things as they might be apart from our assumptions and prejudices. Friedrich was telling us bluntly that our ideas of the world do not mirror the world as it might be apart from our living in it. This must make us re-examine our assumptions about the possibility of knowledge and the nature of reason.

"It seemed to me, as I listened to the learned expositions of René and Immanuel and even of David and Ludwig, at least in his first remarks, that a faith in the autonomy of reason, in the sovereignty of the intellect, its independence of ignorance and special interest, underlies all their thinking. I found myself wondering on what grounds they hold to this faith? Do the results of philosophy warrant it? I can assure you they hardly do in the Sanskrit tradition. Human beings as we know them don't possess an autonomous faculty which penetrates to the nature of things. Each of us generates his philosophy out of a blind ambition to know and an equally blind ocean of inborn, unshakeable, unconscious ignorance, most certainly not out of the divine light of pure reason. Our theories come to us propelled by the forces of a crippled life-potential which we call *karma*, that is, by forces inherited from unenlightened living and thinking in the past. Every attempt to express the truth is therefore doomed to failure, a revelation of the distance one still is from the truth. The very pronouncement of one's truth is the announcement of one's ignorance. I think sometimes that the very intricacies of our best reasoning are the clouds and fog which prevent us seeing the truth.

"I am, as you can see," Nagaraj went on, "strongly sceptical of father Aristos' claim that science discovers the inner nature of the world. The scepticism of your eldest brother is closest to my own and I am thrilled by his vivial approach to philosophical questions; but, if he doesn't mind my saying so, I think he stops just short of the crux. He suspends, as I do, all judgement about external things – he accepts that we cannot know if honey is sweet – but he accepts the incorrigibility of sense impressions. He believes that the *taste* of honey is sweet, but I do not, and on the following grounds. The sweet taste is just as much an object, that is, something named in order to be known, as honey is. That the one is said to be inner and the other outer makes no difference to their nature as named objects of awareness, as entities, so that the same argument brought against the knowledge of 'outer' objects holds equally for 'inner' sense impressions. If we cannot know that honey is sweet, we cannot know that the taste of honey is sweet. In the end, the idea 'entity', a self-existent thing, possessor of qualities which may change but which itself persists unchanged through time, the concept on which the very idea of knowledge rests, is unintelligible. I am forced to think that so grand an idea as knowledge can hardly rest on the unintelligible. We may be sure, at least so I think, that knowledge is not knowledge of entities as René, Immanuel and David so strongly presumed.

"This may at first seem a minor point but I have found it a stumbling block, I would say the critical turn, in my own thinking. Would you, just for a moment, consider some common uses of the notion 'entity'? May I suggest as an example the notion of agent? In some way the notion of agent is integral to our understanding of all process, including our understanding of ourselves as willing, responsible persons. Isn't it so that we commonly accept the notion 'agent' – think of heat melting copper or a thinker producing a thought – as an idea thoroughly intelligible in itself? If it weren't how could it be used in any fixed or intelligible way? But if we step back out of personal involvement in our thinking, that is to say, if we abandon all personal interest in sustaining the conventions of our thinking, it may not be so unambiguous. Is it not so that, to be worthy of the name, an agent must be thought of as *acting* – which is just to put the noun back to back with its own verbal root? That is, an agent that is not acting is not an agent; or, to come closer to my real point, the notion 'agent' *embraces* the notion 'act' and, separated from it, is empty of meaning. Heat that does not *melt* is not the agent we spoke of. A thinker who is not thinking is not the agent we mean when we say 'thinker'. Now it seems that the notion 'act' is no less inseparable from the notion of what the act acts upon or produces – heat melts copper only if copper *becomes* molten; a thinker is thinking only if a thought *arises*.

"These three terms – agent, act and product – used in any intelligible statement about causal processes or human behaviour, seem when critically examined – could I use your great word 'scepsis' here? – not to name self-existent entities. None of the three is an entity whose essence is intelligible in itself. Each of the three terms shows itself to be, on the contrary, so dependent on the other two that only when all three are uncritically held together in the mind does there appear to be any intelligible sense. This is, of course, quite acceptable and effective as an everyday convention, as brother Ludwig has shown us, but it provides no firm basis for a metaphysical theory of entities. I suppose we would all agree that a metaphysical theory, lacking a clear, intelligible base in our hardest thinking, is like a castle in the sky. This is exactly what René had insisted on, even though, as I see it, his own principle 'I think' fails to meet his own criterion. Its terms 'I' and 'think' are not clear, distinct, separate ideas. Each is, taken by itself, as unintelligible as the notions of 'agent' and 'act' were, being but instances of these. How then can they be made sense of taken together? I cannot believe that by adding one unintelligible term to another we achieve good sense, for how could we be sure what a cluster of terms is saying if each single term is unintelligible in itself?

"The collapse of the philosophical and scientific credentials of the concept of entity is in itself crucial for our discussion. But this collapse moves to the dead centre of the problem if we add to it the conundrums that cluster around our attempts to attribute qualities and predicates to alleged entities. Even if the concept of entity still stood, an independent exploration of the way an entity can have a relation to its qualities, or these to it, raises hopeless puzzles. Theories of knowledge, indeed understanding how language can serve the claims of knowledge, turn on seeing this problem unabashed.

"Think of it this way. We say our sun, who seems to have withdrawn for the afternoon, is composed of nuclearly combusting gases in a globular form. So we have 'sun' as subject of the predicates 'globular' and 'nuclearly combusting'. How are we to make the relationship of the sun to its attributes intelligible? How can the sentence 'The sun is composed of nuclearly combusting gases' be made intelligible? Wouldn't we all agree that a subject must first have a nature of its own before any qualities can be attributed to it? Yet it is quite clear that without the burning gases the sun has no nature, is a word, not an entity. So there is no subject for the predicates 'nuclearly combusting' and 'globular' to be predicated of; they hang miraculously in mid air.

Looking at the matter from the other end, it is equally self-evident that attributes are *attributes* only as attributed to something that exists in its own right and stands ready to receive them. Failing such they cease to be attributes. So, if we insist on our everyday understanding of predication we are reduced to accepting the nonsense of a 'subject' which cannot be identified because it has no character, and 'predicates' which, in consequence, belong nowhere and so cannot be used. It won't help, I believe, to object that the word 'sun' is merely a handy name for a huge ball of burning gases, that 'gas' is the real subject. Obviously the identical paradox will break out again. 'Gas' will be unable to exhibit a nature of its own independent of, and so capable of accepting the predicates 'globular' and 'nuclearly combusting'. It seems to me that both terms of the pair 'subject'-'predicate' are, like 'agent,' 'act,' and 'product,' unintelligible in themselves, and so fail to be a basis for the generation of sense in our world.

"Forgive this long, school-teacherly digression. You will now understand, though, why I find the elemental notions 'entity' and 'predication' to be the crux of the question concerning knowledge. The act of predicating some attribute of some entity is the aboriginal act of knowing because it asserts the existence of an intelligible state of affairs. This assertion, commonly buried, is, I believe, the foundation of our sense of the reality of our everyday and scientific worlds. Yet it is, as I have tried to persuade you, an act of faith and practical necessity which is not grounded in its own intelligibility. Must we not then – you will forgive my appearing to be so brash – re-value our vast enterprise of science and philosophy? Whatever their other worths, they will, on my account, fail to realize their claim to *know* even the smallest part of the world we live in.

"David's scepticism was pointed in that direction, though he spoke of causality and not predication, and I liked it as far as it went. However he then offered us belief in place of knowledge; he seemed to believe that believing is immune to the crippling inadequacies of knowledge, whereas, in my view, neither believing nor any other form of rendering things intelligible is so immune. David's belief in belief does not, as I see it, restore respectability to the everyday world, but wraps it once more in obscurity. He fails to attack the notion of reality. Belief must itself be subjected to David's own scepsis.

"Friedrich's denunciation of our everyday and scientific categories – from René's 'I' to Immanuel's 'moral law' to causality in the sciences – as fictions caught my ear too, for that is a good way to make us realize that they are worthless as claimants to knowledge. But in our view they are not fictions in the way that fantasies – rabbits with horns or men with goat bodies – are, not at all. Friedrich's fictions, which make up virtually the entire vocabulary of both the everyday *and* metaphysics – oddly enough all but identical – constitute the everyday world, with whatever reality it must be conceded. We buddhists hold, and this is our wisdom, or, if you like, our ignorance, that even though names do not name self-existent natures – neither substantive nor adjectival – they are not to be rejected as worthless for all purposes. We must live by them, in their web, accepting them as what is given us. They are the mesh of our language and the structure of our everyday world. Without them we have no way of speaking and no world to speak about. To repudiate them we must use them; to talk about what is beyond them – and buddhists like to talk about little else – we must employ them even as we use a pot to hold the water we are drinking.

"No, we cannot do without Friedrich's fictions, but we need not use them unawarely. In their everyday sense they cannot express the truth, for they arouse only delusory expectations. We can make no intelligible statement, that is, no statement which is self-evident through and through, using the fictions of the everyday. The art of thinking, as we try to practise it, lies in using fictions to invoke a sense which is other than verbal intelligibility. Let me say – and I know I shock you – that verbal intelligibility is impossible. However many sentences we link together there is never a completed, self-evident sense in them. To expect there could be is to misconceive the nature of language. The challenge, as we believe, is to find another kind of sense to take the place of intelligibility.

"You can see that in my tradition the world is not a miasma of diseased fictions. It is, rather, the reality in which each of us lives so long as we live without transparencing the fictions, so long as our wisdom eye, as we say, is not opened. The crucial turning point, according to our understanding, is to see that the belief in an external world of substantial entities is inseparable from the belief in ourselves as substantial entities. Which comes first matters little; the two fictions sustain each other reciprocally, like two mirrors each reflecting what the other images. If we are ever to live in a world not choked with impenetrable, solid objects battering each other into patterns of motion, we must learn to see our own inner life as spontaneous activity not controlled by an entity called the self or the ego. Buddhists work at this out of both worlds at the same time, attempting to transparence physical and social entities even while attempting to see through that most bedevilling of all fictions, the personal self. We believe that, if we observe carefully and analyze critically, none of these seeming entities, inner or outer, is ever encountered in our immediate experience.

"René and Immanuel believe that the self is immediately aware of its own reality, whereas we hold the notion of self to be no more true than other notions. It is as necessary as the everyday world is, yet in the end, along with that, it fails to be true, it reveals itself as delusory. I was delighted with David's attack on the reality of the self, but I think he goes too far too fast. It is dangerous to destroy the notion of self before there is a stronger principle to take its place. As some of you may have heard, in my tradition this is the buddha nature or, as we often say, enlightenment, that is, utter innocence. I cannot believe that David's followers, to whom he leaves only sense impressions and probabilities, can be very happy people."

The smiling Nagaraj paused. "I try your patience; forgive me; I am carried away by this first encounter with my illustrious foster brothers. May I try to say one more thing before I leave you to your own thoughts? The overwhelming impression which this wonderful afternoon has made on me is Aristos' hope for an access to the inner nature of the world through knowledge, and for a society of the future founded on the most precise knowledge of human nature and of the laws of the world. The persistence of this hope in your own thinking, in spite of your admirable attempts to sceptically question it, is striking. This is the faith of what was once called metaphysics and what is now, I believe, called science.

"But, leaving aside the usual arguments about the nature of knowledge, even its possibility, can we not ask if man's best way of being with things, or being open to the worth of things, is a way that is as distant, as unfriendly, as demeaning as the way of knowing? Knowing, or what passes for it, is born by the interest of some person who wants to know. Such an interest expresses the tangle of ignorance and ambition that each of us is. So knowing is fated to hit on special aspects of things, and by treating each aspect as real in its own right – self-existent you might say – far from lighting up the true nature of things, it distorts and obscures them.

"It is possible to see the function and importance of knowledge in a different way. Our faith tells us to let things be what they are, apart from the distortions of special interests. What this might be can, of course, never be said in the language of any one special interest, that is, in the language of knowing. That being so it is clearly illegitimate, indeed nonsensical, to speak as if the nature of things could be an object for our knowing. That is why buddhists often say that things, in their truth, are without determinate, entitative natures and so are without names, are unspecifiable. Now, as it is meaningful to say something 'exists' or 'does not exist' only if that something can be specified and named, we try not to use the verb 'to exist' of the true nature of things. We simply repudiate the very notion 'existence' as having no meaning for something which cannot be an object of knowledge. If the true nature of things cannot become an object of knowledge, we hold that it is equally unacceptable to say either that it exists or that it does not exist. We say, and perhaps you will allow me a word from my own language at this point, that the true nature of things is *śūnya.* To say this is to say simply that the truth of things is not a concern of the discipline of knowledge, but of a far different discipline, one I would have to call, if I may so use your language, a life-discipline. The question of the truth of things is a question that properly arises within a greater question: How are we to live with things so that we let them be in their own truth? You have all heard that we buddhists believe it is only the enlightened man who can show us what that way is. I suppose that such a way of thinking must have quite radical consequences for what you traditionally call ontology – the science of being, your noble effort to account for the world within some explanatory system of ideas. Indeed it is not possible for one of us to pursue the question of being, thinking as we do about knowledge and truth.

"Though the significance of things for us in our everyday worlds is limited to their determinate and knowable natures, all things can have, we believe, a significance for one's destiny, for one's life as a whole, for the possibility of enlightenment. I hope it is clear that this is not just one further, even if greater, object of knowledge, that for us there is more to things than the sum of their specifiable aspects.

"Take this maple tree whose cool shade has made this afternoon possible and is, it appears, soon to be our shelter from the storm. In so far as it is classified as *acer saccharum* it 'is' a species of plant within the intricate world of the botanist. In the world of the lumberman it 'is' 'hardwood', usable for furniture or firewood. But call to mind the multitude of other names and uses in virtue of which it takes on significance and existence for us. A maple tree 'is' a visual joy for the painter, it 'is' a subject for his work. With its dense foliage it 'is' the best windbreak for the farmer. It 'is' a heaven-sent jungle gym for the young and a shade from the sun for the old who watch them. Its magical rebirth every spring 'is' a source of wonder for poet and thinker. And for those with a sweet tooth, young or old, it 'is' the source of maple syrup. Let us not forget that it 'is' also a home for nesting birds and for insects and that these are food for the birds and that small rodents eat the tree's seeds when they flutter to the ground. It 'is' at times even a haven for family councils.

"Now what are we to say 'is' the 'tree'? Don't we have to think of it as what effortlessly brings forth this great family of names and uses and benefactions, tolerantly embracing them all, like a mother? The 'tree' is clearly not *acer saccharum*, nor hardwood, nor jungle gym, even though botanist or lumberman or child might take it to be so, for these are names and uses of one or another special aspect and interest. The 'tree' cannot be reduced to any named reality. Nor is it the aggregate of its names and uses. The 'tree', to continue using that word in spite of its rapidly evanescing sense, is more properly its wondrous fecundity, the inexhaustible source of its many functions. 'Source' is a wondrous word, not an explanation, but an evocation of what all explanations need to complete their sense. In its truth this old maple tree speaks the presence of the infinite and the timeless. It is unknowable because outside all contexts and uses.

It is not something to which we can attribute any characteristic commonly thought of as belonging to a tree. The tree in its truth is the presence of the buddha-nature, which is the nature of all beings. So, we understand the 'tree' to be an always possible, available occasion for realizing the truth of all things, which is what we call enlightenment. The tree, in its truth, is *śūnya.*

"In the same way every person and every thing and every living circumstance is, behind a functional, knowable facade, the innocence and the fullness of the buddha nature itself. All things speak the presence of the infinite and the timeless. Every private corner of our lives and every public place of our world is equally the possibility of, and the entrance to, the way of enlightenment. That is their truth, they have no other.

"Ludwig is shaking his head in disbelief. Yet I see a puzzlement in his eye; perhaps his posthumous ideas are not as antagonistic to mine as his earlier ones were. What I am saying must sound strange, even repulsive to you. May I presume to guess why this is? Is it that my way of passing from questions of knowledge to questions of behaviour, or of living, as I would rather say, violates your belief that cognitive functions are autonomous, not to be sullied by lesser concerns? Your reservation would be more than understandable. It is true, buddhists find the ultimate sense of human existence not in theory – whether René's natural reason, Immanuel's moral law or Ludwig's *Lebensform* – not in an intelligible account of things, but in a discipline that transparences both theory and practice.

"It is a discipline not of will and mind only, but one which frees and integrates our feelings, our perceptions, our imaginings, our valuations, our insights so that we may say the whole person speaks with one tongue. And it is a *life*-discipline in that it draws out of, and gives back to every experience a sense which binds the conundrums of human existence into one livable sense. As we see it there is no inner or outer behaviour which cannot light up one's life-sense, and no life-sense which can show itself except as realized in actual living. For buddhists a life-discipline must base itself on a code of behaviour, such as not harming other beings, not lying or stealing. Then there must be a mastery of the mind which results in its calm clarity and its readiness to be used in a deeper understanding of the nature of all life. This in turn makes possible the penetration, in meditation, of the unseen and the deathless – the certainty that human beings have, at their core, the promise of freedom from all the self-inflicted ills of time. We call this certainty awakening or enlightenment. It supervenes only in the practice of the discipline itself, which is inseparably behaviour and understanding.

"Please note, my brothers, that I do not say that in meditation one has an 'intuition' of buddhist liberation or gains an 'insight' into it. That would be theory of knowledge and quite uninteresting for you. No, the carrier of one's sense of life cannot be moments of ecstasy. Why should they be trusted? The only carrier that qualifies is the discipline itself, of whatever kind it may be. Only that opens the door to, and becomes the locus of one's ultimate sense of things, or 'truth' of things – so long as 'truth' is not a theory. In return it is one's ultimate sense of things that informs the discipline. One is not possible without the other. Most of you would believe that a theory is not respectable unless it is true apart from behaviour. I liked brother Chang's wisdom:

'There is no truth until there is a true man.' That is beautiful I think.

"Will you not be too annoyed with me if I tell you that I detect in the philosophy of each of you the seeds of that same wisdom? It slumbers, so to speak, wrapped in epistemological clothing. Can Immanuel not see that his *practical* reason and Friedrich that his subordination of truth to creative living point in this very direction? Your oldest brother most strikingly holds views very close to ours. When he speaks I almost believe it is myself talking. Yet it was Ludwig's graveside musings that took up the question most directly.

"Ludwig, if I understand him fairly, was searching for a ground to everyday thinking and speaking that would replace his earlier faith in logic and its self-evident rules. He believes he found it and the origin of our religious and moral beliefs as well in our culturally rooted behaviour. It is now clear to him that we must concede priority to behaviour, not to rules of thinking. In the end, he said, it is our way of life that gives meaning to our speech, which is just the view we buddhists hold. But of course Ludwig cannot concede that ways of behaving are the opening into a truth which is a life-truth. He moves forward from culturally determined ways of behaving, from some *Lebensform* as he puts it to himself, into the jungle of conventional, everyday ways of thinking. He attempts no more – please excuse that ungrateful expression, it is a great thing he has done – than to show that our logics of reasoning themselves lack a logical foundation. Why do I sense a sadness in him? Perhaps he longs to penetrate the empirical origins of our thinking but is prevented by his own integrity from finding an acceptable way to do that?

"So you see we have the possibilities of moving each others' thought forward. This question of a discipline to secure the good sense of all life is, I think, the crux of what your father said, it seems so long ago, at the beginning of this momentous afternoon. He said scepticism will issue in nihilism if some principle is not found to take the place of cognitive truth. What prescience! That is exactly, it seems to me, what we have discovered in our explorations. Some form of life-discipline has been offered as just that fresh principle.

"It is clear to me that what I have just said is the strongest message I can bring you. It requires other horizons of sense than your philosophical tradition allows. It would force open the powerful doors you have always built in the halls of what can make sense. Its testing would require a long descent into the past in search of the origins of your belief that only the intelligible can be accepted as possessed of sense. We find that sense is closer to life than the intelligible and more embracing. Theories are splendid thrusts into possible ways of behaving toward or manipulating the world of things. But, as they burgeon, theories hide from us and suffocate the tender shoots of good sense lying close around them.

"I realize I have but tentatively dipped one of my toes in a vast problem. But I felt I had to tell you that the difference between Aristos' philosophy and our way of thinking is not a difference between two theories. It is the difference between the sovereignty of theory and the sovereignty of life-sense. Our descendants will have to face this clash nakedly. How can or will theory yield to life-sense without losing the great benefactions of the philosophic and scientific adventure?

"I must break off, I am beginning to preach. But before I release you from your courteous attentiveness I would like to give you my farewell reflection. I have long been haunted by an uncanny thought about human existence, and this afternoon has revived it almost painfully. It will not leave me in peace.

"The uncanny thought arises when it strikes home that, though we pass our lives profoundly sure that our speech names things which we can come to know, in the truth of enlightenment this is seen to be untrue. We realize that, in the buddha-awakening, *nothing* of our everyday life is any longer as we so dogmatically believed it to be. The uncanny thought which arises is quite simple, but devastating. It is that the entire, vast panorama of the everyday world is one living tapestry of delusion, a dream you might say, or a magic show. If the rock-hard realities of people and things, of money and war, of passions and pain can dissolve in front of our very eyes, without an act of will on our part, as gently as an idea dissolves in the mind, and in no time at all – such is the account given of enlightenment – and if that dissolution doesn't destroy realities but transparences their truth, their buddha nature, what can one say but that life in the everyday is a dream or a magic show?

"To say this is not to offer you a philosophical theory, because it doesn't attempt to explain anything. Explaining would be like washing a clod of earth in a mud bath, to borrow a saying from Chang's people. It is simply the voice of our discipline. The buddha-awakening puts an end to the reality of the everyday by revealing it as a dream or a magic show. We can't claim to *know* this in your sense of cognition, obviously; but it has been tested many times and always the awakened ones say 'My life was a dream, now the dream has vanished, and there is only the buddha's truth.'

"So, you see, thought moves in many ways, not all comprehended within your illustrious father's horizon. I suppose our way will be puzzling to you and may seem irrelevant. But you were kind enough to ask an alien for his views, and now you have heard that we buddhists – and many other Sanskrit thinkers as well – are not bound to the same faith as the sons of Aristos have been. And yet you who are here this afternoon are close to my own heart in your fearless and sceptical reflections on your father's work. Your earnest philosophies and great learning are a joy to me. I hope we may gather in our family circle many times yet again."

Nagaraj stopped speaking, folded his hands to his forehead, hitched up his robe and settled back in his lotus composure, as fresh as before he had begun his assault on Aristos' philosophy.

Silence around the circle.

The storm, which had become more threatening while Nagaraj spoke, was now directly overhead. Black, thunderous clouds and shafts of lightning fought for the heavens; but the rain, falling straight down, seemed only to cool and refresh. The tree itself moved quietly as if enjoying the storm, and spread its ease to the men below.

And still silence around the circle.

In the silence Nagaraj's simple thoughts echoed as questions in the thinking of the others:

Names do not name?

All claims to knowledge are disclosures of ignorance?

Every verbal statement is, in the end, unintelligible?

Words serve primarily to evoke and guide behaviour?

Language weaves unintelligible notions into the warp and woof of a delusory world?

Language can be used to repudiate the claims of language?

Knowing things is not the best way of being with things?

Truth is not the concern of knowledge but of a life-discipline?

A wise man can speak so as to transparence ordinary speech?

All things and situations, though not fictions, are śūnya, *fàcades of their own truth, entrances to the middle, the awakened way?*

The everyday world is a dream, a magic show?

Thus the disquieting resonance of Nagaraj's thoughts for the brothers. And each realized: this is more disturbing than the most radical scepticism. This withdraws reality from the everyday world. This compels a re-thinking to the very roots of our profoundest beliefs and most ancient and favoured assumptions about the structure of this universe and the destiny of human beings in it. This emasculates science and threatens philosophy itself. It threatens morality. It threatens common sense. It threatens sanity.

And each thought: there is, of course, a certain force in these ideas within the safety of the buddhist faith. But do they retain that force outside of buddhism? It may be that some of Nagaraj's paradoxes are inescapable; indeed similar suspicions have been ghosting in the background of our own thinking for some time. But is there hope of resolving them in a way that is not buddhist or religious in some sense? The Buddha's one-time awakening is irrelevant to us and to the problem. Can Nagaraj's idea of a life-discipline as the way an ultimate sense of life discloses and sustains itself be accepted into philosophy? Or does it destroy philosophy? Does it overthrow our hallowed faith in reason, on which the very possibility of philosophy is founded?

And each had a final doubt: can we say 'all is dream, a magic show' when the awareness of this thought cannot itself be part of that dream or magic show? Does the argument not collapse in self-contradiction?

For each and all of the great men these gnawing doubt-questions gathered like so many harsh discords in the echo of Nagaraj's words, turning their thinking back onto the proud doctrines they had once given to the world in the shadow of their father's teaching. The alchemy of thought began its work of metamorphosis. Doubt eased into wonder. Ancient horizons of presumption – the unacknowledged guarantors of the gnoseal faith and boundaries of the conceivable – since classical times hidden in the oblivion of the obvious, emerged into a new focus of awareness. And dissolved at once into questions of themselves, questions that opened out onto new fields where there were as yet no horizons. Unthinkable thoughts began to stir. New paradoxes fused with old doctrines in uncanny wonderment.

The anchors of existence loosened for each of the brothers as he commenced the agony of exploring, alone in silent soliloquy, whither his thinking must now tend.

After The Storm

Metamorphosis

René

The dissonance "Names do not name," echoed from the doctrine "I think, therefore I am."

Names of everyday perishables like wax candles and altar pieces do not refer to unchanging essences. This much is quite obvious and was even insisted on in my earlier works. But now, if this is to hold not merely for objects of the senses but as well for the inner life, for the objects of reason, then names like "thinking" and "thinking being" will not name anything. Nor will, God forbid, even the name "god" name anything, and mathematical realities will not be safe. What seemed a self-evident factum – one's own thinking – will, whatever it might turn out to be, not be the pure and unique activity that the name "thinking" led one to believe it was. In this sense, what were taken to be the hard, self-evident facts of the inner life and the sure steps of reasoning – the foundation of a new principle of the sciences – would become delusory, a complex seeming. The confident pronouncement "I am" will not name the reality of one's own existence and "ego" will not name oneself. One would become a collage of floating names. This would destroy the basis of all science and of moral and religious life as well.

It seems too improbable. Our every waking moment speaks against it. We live in the element of "I am" and of familiar, named things. Nothing would be left us if names were taken away. But . . . hold on. The new paradox did not deny this. It told that names are precisely the substance and comfort of our everyday worldly home. We live in, with and by them. It is just that they are not the language of truth. They are not to be taken in the naive, literal way in which they offer themselves.

Well and good. But how are we to take them? How can we think our way around this great stumbling block? What truth can do without names? Well . . . yes, there is a possibility coming to mind that is as yet nameless.

If it can be said that names fail to name realities, then clearly there is an awareness of this failure and there must be some sense of what it is that is present and gives itself as real but which cannot be named. This awareness of the failure of names will have to be other than the awareness for which names name realities or it could never discern the limitations of names and repudiate them sweepingly. Ergo, there *is* an inner life. It is that, in this new way, the names "I," "think," "am," "doubt," "reason," and so on, do not yield *knowledge* of an inner life. They *point at* important features of it even while misleading us into the belief that our inner life is composed of realities which correspond one-for-one to these and other such names. The awareness and repudiation of a belief in names discloses, we were told, an unsuspected inner life which, even though it cannot be known through words, and just because it cannot, is closer to one and less open to doubt than "I think" and

"I am" ever were. Transparencing the names allows what the names covered up to come closer, to become a new "reality," or, more properly, a new truth.

But, how am I to conceive what was concealed by the words "I am" if it was not the existence of my own ego? Granted, "I am" may not be a defensible scientific statement. Still, it is the pristine, unmediated, unpremeditated, natural way of taking the voice from one's own inner depths. I am still puzzled how subsequent reflection and a theory of language can annul such unquestionable certainty. And yet they do unseat it. There is much to be thought about here.

But again, what of my earlier doctrine that, from the self-evident clarity of "I think, therefore I am" our natural reason can proceed, step by sure step, to infer the existence of god and so secure our religious beliefs? This is brought into question by the new thought that reason has no unquestionable foundation, no rock-hard realities with names, to proceed from. Worse still, the strange new dictum "Every verbal statement is unintelligible" would make the pronouncements of reason unconvincing in any case. We would not be able to reason our way from experience – even from the most immediate experience – to a first cause, an all powerful creator. It would be futile. It would be fatuous to believe that any religious faith can be secured by reason. Does this mean there can be no more religious philosophy? Undoubtedly. But does it mean that religious beliefs and practices must be proscribed? It was said "Words serve primarily to evoke and guide behaviour." What if this can be turned toward our religious life? What if religious and moral *thinking* are the language of spiritual *behaviour*? Improbable it seems, but what a prospect! Impossible to comprehend at once. Is this the way religious thought will have to move if these new radical doubts take root?

My doubts remain. Can mankind continue to believe in divine beings while seeing clearly that such are mere fictions? Friedrich wanted them to be *unusable* fictions, deserving only to be discarded. But that would be the end of a divine presence among us. Creative life-force, eternal return, superhuman beings; these are not the substance of religion. Besides, they are as much fictions as my words were: they are simply Friedrich's preferred fictions. Nagaraj held more possibilities open even if they were not Christian. We will have to find some way to preserve the spontaneous sincerity of religious practices even in this new sceptical world.

And, what of the mechanical processes of nature? They seem so understandable, so assured by the explanations of scientific reasoning. Certainly for the practical purposes of experiment and engineering they will stand, but can they any longer be taken as literal descriptions of external reality? If names do not name, if language weaves unintelligible notions into the wearable garments of scientific thinking, then our 'rational' explanations of natural events will have to be seen as a special kind of complex thinking behaviour, not as the fruit of cognition through reason. And that means that, when taken to be literal descriptions, rational accounts of the mechanisms of nature become delusory, a kind of unaware pretence. Ludwig, surprisingly, in his final remarks offered some support for this heresy. He was content to be sure that logical argument was grounded, not in logical principles, but in deeply ingrained speech-behaviour dispositions. He came close to agreeing with

Nagaraj. All this is forcing me to see that my earlier attempt to establish the authority of reason in science and religion was hasty and unfounded and not the best of reasoning.

Yet, the natural scientists in their laboratories and the mathematicians in their studies will have to *believe* that they are working with realities or else their efforts will be something like sleepwalking. Perhaps Nagaraj's thought need not hold for practical undertakings?

But all this is too much for one time. I must begin to wonder what I did to philosophy with my confident young man's doubting of all tradition. It seemed so natural, so reasonable then. Now I see that we are all on the same long, sceptical slope sliding into the abyss of unreason, of unknowing.

Immanuel

The dissonance "All claims to knowledge are disclosures of ignorance," echoed from the thought, "The thing-in-itself only *appears* to the human understanding, and appearance is the sole sphere of human knowledge."

If this new thought holds, then the categories of the everyday and scientific worlds – causality, necessity, existence and so on – not only do not tell us what things are in themselves, as I have always maintained, but cannot yield knowledge even of appearances. Now this undermines what I had earlier thought. The categories we think with would have to be seen as useful ways of observing the behaviour of, but not of knowing, the appearances of the everyday and of the laboratory. If, as Nagaraj suggested, the category "thing" or "entity" is unintelligible, the entire weight of scientific explanation can no longer be based on such a notion. For it is not entity merely as external, substantial thing – sun, moon, or atomic particle – that has been repudiated, but also the self-nature of what concepts like "energy," "force," "field," refer to. If the scientific claim to know such appearances is to be ignorance, how far removed from mortal capability must be the thing-in-itself, which can never be encountered even as appearance! Indeed, if the notion of entity is beyond the pale of intelligible discussion, then whatever lies behind appearances can no longer be thought of as a thing, even if graced by the saving phrase "in-itself." It would have to be thought of in some other way.

Nagaraj challenged us to see that categories are a substitute for knowledge, and, though not error as such, marks of human ignorance; to see that they embody the failure of knowledge. This shocks one and undermines our tradition, so we will want to fight back. But in one sense it is not wholly without promise. Because, if there is awareness that scientific categories, as claims to knowledge, express ignorance, this will be the clearest evidence that there must be someone, or a somewhat, demanding more than scientific facts and scientific explanations to satisfy our longing for certainty and sense.

Something close to this was being got at in what I expounded earlier about practical reason and the true self of each person. "Suprasensible being" was the name used for one's true being – "soul," as is commonly said – the thing-in-itself behind the drama and play of the passing contents of the mind. It seemed certain to me that the self of each person *exists* suprasensibly although we can never have any certainty about the *nature* of this self. Now if names are held not to name any entity, but mark our ignorance, then, of course, the expression "self" does not name anything and so conveys no knowledge, and the expression "exists" will be equally vacuous and illegitimate. It will no longer be possible to say that one *knows* that "one" "exists."

This is persuasive as an argument, even though, when put into plain words, it becomes grotesquely paradoxical and downright impossible. The certainty that there is something in the inner life of a person that is not a mere named-item of the everyday world – a passing feeling, idea or perception – is as involuntary and unshakeable as ever. But to believe that that "something" can be known as *oneself*, and to believe that to say it *exists* is true, would be what Nagaraj meant by ignorance. I can see his point. The trouble is it would be equally true for the ideas of practical reason: "freedom," "god" and "immortality." Such great words, however inspiring, would not be able to continue to make any claim to convey an intelligible idea, for nothing could correspond to them essentially. Even to claim that they are not objects of knowledge but merely necessary postulates of practical reason – that is, of moral behaviour – will no longer satisfy this new way of thinking. What could it mean to believe reason was postulating "freedom," "god," "immortality" if these words refer to nothing? Can one postulate nothings?

Nagaraj, like a skillful dentist, draws my teeth with the weakest roots. Can I any longer ignore the criticism that to believe that the postulates of behaviour are given by a universally binding practical reason is a confusion of thought and a delusion? Of course David and Friedrich both attacked the suprasensible self, but not so compellingly. David attacked me for not being able to point to the inner perception on which the idea of a self is based. But, of course, as what I mean by self is precisely not found amid the manifold of our perceptions, his criticism, interesting as it is, remains empty. Practical reason is not subject to the conditions governing perceptual appearances.

Friedrich attacked with all the power of a battleship,

if not with the precision of a marksman. He charges, with David, that there is no empirical evidence of a single self. He says he is many selves, all deriving from the life that lies unnoticed beneath the surface of our conscious minds. I gather that Friedrich would have us believe that whatever from this source takes over and dominates our lives is the nearest a human can ever come to a true self. I admire the artist in him, but he remains caught in the manifold of the sense world. He was not able to undermine, except by calling it an unusable fiction, the equally strongly given factum of the moral consciousness – the pure voice of a self above the sense world. Nagaraj is the most compelling because he agrees with me that the decisive domain for humans is suprasensible. More, he offers an understanding of it less dependent on protracted argument than my own has been. I do now see that I must test my previous postulates of reason again. They may not be the sure support of religious doctrines in the way I first announced them to be.

And the moral law, the great "factum" as I called it, which was to be the one certain bridge from the world of the senses, of the everyday, to the suprasensible, from appearances to the thing-in-itself, the guarantee that man belongs to an order beyond the natural order, it too is assaulted in this stormy encounter. It too would have to be labelled ignorance in the guise of knowledge. The moral law, I must now agree, surreptitiously clung to the last hope of knowledge in metaphysical matters. It implied that we may be, in some vague gnoseal sense, certain that there *is* freedom and that there *is* god and that there *is* immortality, even though, as was admitted, we have no knowledge, in my own precise sense, of these great matters, and even though this certainty obtains only within the sphere of morality. I feel pushed, reluctantly, to agree that this surreptitious invocation of the prestige of knowledge will have to be acknowledged and given up. The language of morality cannot henceforth be taken as the voice of reason; it can no longer be understood as naming suprasensible realities. The dictum "Words serve to evoke and guide behaviour" may come to have its primary application in matters of morals and religion. For it is there that the ideas of reason – the moral structure of human life – could be understood to hold open a domain for total life responses to what is beyond the senses.

Ludwig's last thoughts were germane to this problem. But I fear I shall never be able to make much of his language empiricism, of the way he buries reasonable argument in the unreason of cultural habit. Reason slips between his fingers and he is left with the mere given practices of historical cultures. Nagaraj at least recognized an ineluctable suprasensible behind empirical conventions.

All this raises a new problem. If the voice of practical reason – the indubitable oracle of the moral law – is henceforth to be denied a comprehensible language, if its terms are evocative and conductal but not something to be comprehended, how will men ever be sure they have understood its imperatives? What can conceivably be the means of understanding between a suprasensible imperative which in its purity comes to us unworded, and the everyday person whose maxims must be worded if they are to be enacted? Fascinating problems. But without faith, very difficult.

This certainly turns one's head. But I worry.

Something must be given us – inwardly or outwardly – to see, to know, to be sure of, if there is to be any foundation for reasoning and behaviour to build on. Nagaraj has dissolved the everyday ingeniously but has left us unable to grasp how ideas and words seize hold of anything real. His "life-discipline" as the carrier of life-sense still leaves the cognitive function of ideas and words quite obscure. He owes us much yet. Or perhaps we owe ourselves much ruthless thought yet.

The words of Nagaraj silently resounded on around the seated circle.

David

The dissonance "Every verbal statement about the world is, in the end, unintelligible" echoed from the earlier thought "Reason cannot see into the connection of causality between objects."

Causality is unintelligible; that much is clear and was insisted on earlier. But what of the notions "idea," "impression," "habit," "imagination," "belief"? These were offered in substitute, as it were, of the principle of causality; and certainly in the belief that they yielded intelligible explanations of events. But if these preferred notions name no realities, no entities, if their gnoseal claim is worth nothing, if they must be unintelligible along with all verbal statements, if they convey the pretence of knowledge but are delusory, then the sceptics are more nearly right than I thought.

It was perhaps hasty to dismiss scepticism as a malady humans can rid themselves of only by turning their backs on. It is now clear that this missed the point. Scepticism jolts the everyday mind, indeed even the philosophical mind, to a full stop by flashing the nonsense character of the world, a nonsense world because all things facade as sense, but, on examination, reveal themselves to be unintelligible. This is not a technical point made within a theory of knowledge. It is a jolt which makes us ask what point there can be in attempting theories of knowledge at all. Because it attacks our presumption of the reality of things, of a world of docile objects waiting to be known, it makes all theories of knowledge irrelevant.

Still, through all his deft attacks on knowledge and reasoning, Nagaraj was trying to persuade us by processes of reasoning and on the presumption of knowledge that we had no good reason to trust in reason. How can the sceptic make use of the rules and language of reason and logic and by that very use demonstrate that they do not exist? This conumdrum will dog us for a long time yet. There must be something basic but simple that has eluded me so far. I can quite understand that Nagaraj's unconditional scepsis is not an alternate theory of knowledge. I can see that it is a life stance quite outside all epistemology. It impels men to a search for new ways of thinking in a topsy turvy world where traditional reason is no longer judge and jury. But I do not see how it can be fruitful within our family tradition.

Nagaraj is a shock, certainly. But more shocking still was the way Friedrich, of his own inspiration, opened the door to this new thinking by attacking the basic presumptions of our family tradition. He threw knowledge, truth and reality bodily out the front door, even though, in disguise, they crept back in through a rear entrance. But then to hear Ludwig retreat from his logical positivism into a cultural relativism which seemed to extend even to mathematics and the rules of reasoning! What is happening? We seem to be moving more and more deeply into the forests of scepsis where Nagaraj is waiting to greet us. Is this the ironic destiny of our father's philosophy? And how will we be able to develop a new science of man?

Friedrich

The dissonances, "Language weaves unintelligible notions into the warp and woof of a delusory world," "Words serve primarily to evoke and guide behaviour," "All things are but the facade of their own truth" struck an echo from the metaphysics of a creative power that dwells in all things, eternally re-creating the worlds.

Yes, it had always been clear that every metaphysic, every world-structuring notion fails in its intention to convey knowledge and, claiming to be what it is not, is to that extent delusory. So, as was suspected though not always openly conceded, and as Nagaraj has made crystal clear, the notions "eternal return" and "creative power" did not yield knowledge of the world. They were and are, gnoseally, fictions. The notion "creative power," maladroitly taken as "will to power" – the belief that the final resting place of man's thoughtful search for sense must be with the notion of the spontaneously creative force that dwells in and moves all things in good or in bad – was not, in spite of its pretensions, a metaphysical theory. I can now see more clearly that this was my attempt to find a new principle of human behaviour. "Creative power" was, without my realizing it, an evocative and ductal naming on the way to the discovery of that creative source from which men could draw substance for their thought and conduct. Too easily all of us, and certainly I did so myself, halted at the *name* "creative force" and mistook it for the substance of the discovery.

And "eternal return," the notion that man's fullest power, his innocence, is possible only if the past and the future are given the dignity and worth of the present, only if he lives in present time as eternal time, was, likewise, not a theory about time and the world, though I tried hard to make it into one. I did not always understand this and certainly did not consistently admit it. "Eternal return" was meant to be the naming of a new stoicism, a summons to a new stance in the modern wasteland. It was an heroic poem, my lived answer to nihilism. It was, if confusedly, an evocative and ductal naming, not a gnoseal one.

However, the notion that the nature of man was not formed once and for all time but is capable of radical mutation, was acknowledged from the beginning to be, not an historical prognosis, but a call to action. The notion that further moral and intellectual development of the human species – the transhumanizing of the human, hopelessly distorted as "superman" – is the condition of the survival of the species was my dare to live with the creative power in all things, as with oneself.

The mists of centuries are dissipating. It is clear now. All world-structuring notions, all philosophical concepts, though delusory if pretending to convey knowledge, can, if used wisely, be entrances to a way of living – whether Nagaraj's middle way, or my way of eternal return or what other way so ever. I once said, "All things are baptised in the well of eternity." That was close to Nagaraj's dictum "All things are the facade of their own truth" and to his explanation that all things and situations are entrances to his buddhist middle way. "Middle way," "eternity," "creative force" will be simply different names for the unworded source of the sense men have of the truth of things. Without this source, this dumb sense of truth, men wouldn't be able to speak at all, but they can't speak directly about it at all either.

An even stronger thought closes in. To say all things can speak the truth but man cannot looses a thunderbolt into the mind. It jolts all explanation, every effort to render things intelligible, to a stop. It dissipates the hope of *knowing* a final truth. It closes out the millennial enterprise of metaphysics. It puts an end to the notion that knowing can be an adequate way of relating to whatever is the source and sustenance of human life. This much our buddhist brother told us.

He did not, however – there was no occasion to do so – follow the course of his own thinking beyond this point. If this longing for a self-evident sense of all things need not be bound to objects merely as their docile description, it may, as a human form of creativity – however much it remains the voice of powers above and below the human – surge universes beyond what acquaintance with objects can tell us. Then we joyfully realize that human thinking helps to *build* the world men must live in, that its purpose is to do just that.

This is no longer buddhism. It is no longer philosophy. We will have to hold unequivocally that man's truth is not the truth about a world someone else made, but is the substance of the world he is making for himself. We will have to hold unequivocally that man's truth – the way he deals with the things and ideas about him, and his sciences and philosophies and religions and value systems – is sustained by a sense of truth which is beyond man's ability to speak sensibly about. This may be taken for nonsense but it is more like an invitation to join a magic show.

Not simple magic but triple magic.

It is magic enough, for one thing, that the foundation of the world is not of the same substance as the things of the world, that mere truth, insubstantial, can bear the grotesque weight of the massive universe effortlessly. It is, further, magic that things can effectively pretend a truth they don't have, that they sustain the spell of everyday reality eternally. Thricely, it is magic that this magic, when taken as the sense of life as Nagaraj does, can become transparent as light. Triple magic.

But will philosophers be able to make sense of magic, a very unphilosophical term? Nagaraj's thinking, leaving out his religious buddhism of course, is close to my own. Indeed he awakens me to further reaches of my own ideas. I was trying, by myself, to hatch out of the old philosophical egg and couldn't see that large pieces of shell were still sticking to my ideas. But the philosophical spell we are living under is very strong and naturally inhospitable to magic. I can see now that we will need thinkers of a new vision. The excitement lies ahead. There are so many dawns that have not yet shed their light.

In the growing calm the great maple stretched its limbs.

Ludwig

The harsh paradox "Language can be used to repudiate the claims of language," echoed from the thought "When language is used apart from its everyday origins we talk nonsense."

From the first the crippling paradox, that language was, at one and the same time, within itself and beyond itself, haunted the investigations into the nature and limits of language. Indeed it was hesitatingly admitted that the analysis of everyday uses of words could proceed only from an understanding of these everyday uses which itself was not an everyday usage. But I did not openly accept the haunting implications of this paradox. No escape from language to nature was permitted and no other escape was recognized, so no way of becoming aware of language from a vantage point outside of language was provided for, even though my investigations were conducted from just such a vantage point. Only the bare fact that we become aware of the uses and rules of language, of the existence of what were called "language games," and that we knew we were so aware, was admitted. Any attempt to penetrate into this surrounding awareness, itself outside language, was repudiated out of hand. Indeed, the possibility of doing so was ignored.

But if now this strange capacity of language to lend itself to talk about itself – this incipient transcendence, to use the traditional vocabulary – is taken seriously, there will be consequences. Language will no longer be a self-limiting, autocratic realm of logical relationships to be described from within like a beehive or a fine machine. The sense of words and statements will have to be seen to derive from what is itself not language. No longer can I arbitrarily relegate certain kinds of pronouncement to the limbo of nonsense.

There is now the question of a criterion. From where do we draw our sense of what makes sense and what doesn't? The appeal will have to be to what is beyond language. Then overt self-contradiction will no longer be *eo ipso* inadmissible. To say "Language can repudiate language" or "The only truth is that there is no truth" need not be excluded from language. Indeed such jolting nonsense will tell us much about the nature of sense, will tell us that verbal nonsense need not rule out profound sense. I may even have to accept a new principle: the rules governing language are not rules *of* language. That would mean that we cannot expect worded sentences to be intelligible through and through. The wonder will be that we can make any sense out of what is verbally unintelligible.

Nagaraj's claim that a wise man can speak so as to transparence ordinary speech is a direct attack on my earlier thought that language games are meaningful only within everyday usage. If words can be used with sense, even if only by a wise man, in those remote reaches of experience and thought where the magic of enlightenment is supposed to strike, then our criterion of sense and nonsense cannot always be found in the everyday habitat of the words being used. The right man would be able to say "The middle way says neither yea nor nay" and the sense of this statement would not be confined within the everyday uses of "middle," "way," "yea," and "nay." This is not an everyday use of language. It claims the right to be tested in the remotest regions of the discipline – contemplative, philosophical, religious – where it is integral to the inner behaviour enjoined. There it can be used to fulfil a certain purpose well understood by those involved, so it is claimed.

If such a statement does, within the given discipline, evoke and guide inner behaviour, then it will have to be admitted that it indeed has good sense. This train of thought, if I follow it through, will constrain me to admit that statements from regions as remote as religious belief and philosophical doctrine are just as integral to the special inner behaviour of those regions as everyday statements are to the common tasks of the everyday. I will have to admit that the words which evoke and guide behaviour in the furthest reaches of the mind are as full of sense, for those who inhabit such spheres, as the language of the hockey coach is for those who play hockey. The sensible use of language will extend just as far as language is effectively used. Language games, from the carpenter's workbench to the saint's ecstasy, can all be seen as one in being attempts to find a worded way in an unworded world.

But the long reach of Nagaraj's strange words, and indeed of Friedrich's and the elder brother's, is not fully acknowledged in these cogitations. Even my later thinking feels their impact. Let me summon my graveside honesty. The sentence "Every verbal statement is, in the end, unintelligible" is more radical than I had dared to be when I said that our basic beliefs about the world and our principles of logic are without ground in reason, being merely judgements. The implications of the more radical thought cannot be ignored. All speech, even though efficacious, is said not to be intelligible through and through. Common talk is intelligible in that we weave it more or less effortlessly into our actions, but that does not make it intelligible through and through, does not ensure it an intelligible ground. Speech merely appears to be intelligible because we have no everyday need to unearth its unintelligible substrata.

This must be accepted now with its consequences. To put inherited and acquired speech-behaviour in place of rational origins as the bedrock of everyday language was a natural move for one of my background. And there was some support for this in Nagaraj's sentence "Language serves primarily to evoke and guide behaviour." But that is not the end of the matter. It was important to me to see not only that speech – promises, questions, pronouncements – evokes and guides behaviour, but also that we don't know what anyone has in truth *said* until they have lived out their own words, it may be years later. Our behaviour gives the full meaning to our words. This was meant to be radical. Nagaraj's dictum "A wise man can speak so as to transparence ordinary speech," which he clarified by saying that the middle way replaces the meaning of a wise man's words – indeed *is* their meaning – goes beyond my empirical account. Nagaraj wants speech to become transparent so that it no longer obscures and distorts the truth, but discloses it – his "middle way." That echoes unconvincingly from our time. Yet both Friedrich and the elder brother said much the same thing, minus only the buddhist dogma. Someone must come to terms with this.

The great discovery of my later years was the inevitability of unexamined presumptions in every reasoning inquiry. I came to see that thinking can proceed only as it does not become aware of any principles which might put its progress in doubt. I came to believe that this unaware self-deception was integral to philosophical thinking. I said that this unspeakable background was perhaps what gave some meaning to what we do say.

When Nagaraj told us that our very sense of the *reality* of the everyday was just such an unaware presumption normally immune to doubt, I realized, again, that we were being challenged to a more radical re-thinking of human existence than we would be capable of within our own tradition. There is the possibility that humans, due to some inherent crippling – *karma* or thrall or whatever it might be – are incapable of facing the world without a deep distortion. Simple thought, but with quaking consequences. Away would go the sacred "given" of empiricist explanations; away would go my own view that historical-cultural circumstance is a grounded starting point for thought about humans.

How to proceed? No explicit arguments have been offered against the referral of our prejudices and primary judgements to the cultural milieu in which they are acquired, and within which they serve as the basis of our thinking and behaviour. So there is no reason to rethink this view. Yet I must. There is a dis-ease in the thought that nothing more need be said. Is a point in cultural history, which must be arbitrary, the best absolute our philosophy can offer?

If it is, why have I been haunted for so long by the awareness that beyond our thought-worlds there is something superhuman, something supranatural, which bounds our understanding but which is utterly beyond its reach? The earlier thought "Only the supranatural can express the supranatural" appears now, in this moment of soliloqual honesty, as a trite tautology, quite useless. In the echo of Nagaraj's confidence that the everyday is the home of the infinite, how can we crudely cleave things into two halves – the natural and the supranatural? The very terms bind themselves together. Nagaraj holds that it is possible to transparence natural things and let the supranatural shine through. My semitic roots will not be pulled up quite so easily and yet I said myself before the storm that all our philosophic reasoning remains mere linguistic skill lacking lasting worth, unless and until it is illuminated by a light which comes from outside one's own self. What is that light if not at least a brother to Nagaraj's buddha truth that, as he says, shines through a wise man's words?

What is it that blocks acceptance of the hidden light, the unspeakable depthground of our reasoning? Why do we in our time find this thought so repugnant, so impossible to grasp in seriousness? Words do become lexically and syntactically absurd if we try to talk sense about it. No doubt at all. And so we despair and exercise our contempt. But if, as I now see, words *spring from* behaviour, why could they not also find their *fulfillment* in behaviour? Why could language and aware behaviour not be so closely interwoven that neither was the exclusive locus of sense? This would fit with Nagaraj's notion of a life-discipline. This would re-cast the problem of making intelligible *statements* about the supranatural, and so would topple verbal intelligibility from its position at the head of the totem pole. What a thought. Why can I not move toward that undertaking? What invisible chains hold me back? Have the cultural-historical origins of *my* beliefs forever removed the possibility of my talking about such matters?

Around the silent circle the soliloqual brooding moved on as the benevolent rumblings of the storm drew off to the west.

Chang

The sentences "Names do not name," "All claims to knowledge are disclosures of ignorance" and "The everyday world is a dream, a magic show" echoed sympathetically from the ancient belief in the true man, the oneness of all things and the great tao.

These ancient beliefs were indeed commanding thoughts and true in some sense. But Nagaraj has now made it seem that their strength, their special certainty which gave itself to be the certainty of knowledge was founded on a natural delusion, even though their effect was truly vivial. Their seeming ability to yield an irreducible understanding of human destiny, that is, to be true, was, he pointed out, justified not logically but vivially, in the Taoist life-discipline. Nagaraj constrains us to see our ancient beliefs as admonitions about the way humans should live, not as cognitive claims.

Ludwig anticipated this in some degree. But as he could invoke nothing more illuminating than the circumstances of culture as explanation, he left a great abyss of problems unprobed. Nagaraj clarified much of what was implicit in our own thinking and I can now accept the weight of what he said. But a new puzzlement arises. How can a mere human be sure what the admonitions, the messages of the life-discipline, vivial pointings which speak to one without words, are admonishing and pointing to? How be sure that the unentangled man of the tao is more "true" than the socially dutiful confucian man? How be sure that the vivial oneness of all things in the tao is more true than the intricate bonds and rituals of society? How can we be sure what ideas are being whispered into our inner ear if the message does not come to us in names? How can we be sure what behaviour is enjoined, even in which direction to move?

The consequence of this namelessness is that the man of thought should no longer insist that he *knows* what the message is, for knowing has need of names. He will not even know how to set about finding out what it might mean. He will see that everyone must live out of the certainty that *his* reading of the unworded message is right, that *he* knows what it is saying to him and therefore what is "true". He will see too, and equally clearly, that this certainty can never be founded in knowledge. In this new way of thinking men will be able, at most, to release themselves from the half-truths and delusions of conventional society by listening more carefully to their spontaneous feelings and ideas before they become paralyzed in words. At most they will find in the unclouded thought and natural heart a way of letting all things, including themselves, be in their own best ways. This new thought looks like its own kind of dogmatism, as of course it must, even though it is not a dogmatism of argument but more an encouragement to a basic stance in the world. Odd that, even so, it retains its own kind of certainty.

This new certainty rests on the certainty that grammatical truths are not formulations of knowledge, not descriptions of reality, even though they appear to be so, but are vivial exhortations, conductal empowerments. It will seem to us taoists that, for most men, this insight will have to carry the authority of knowledge if it is to sustain the faith that it expresses. What a delightful and ironic paradox! Faith in non-knowledge forced to take on the protective appearance of knowledge! We know that we do not know! Two certainties, equally indispensable, each nullifying the other. This lies outside the intelligible. This is like a dream or a conjuror's act. If it is not too difficult for us it may allow human life a new grace and a new dignity. We will see.

And the tree above swayed gently.

The Brother From Elis

The pronouncements "Knowing things is not the best way of being with things" and "Truth is not the concern of knowledge but of a life-discipline" echoed back in rich discords from the oldest of the sceptical thoughts: Knowledge being impossible, suspension of judgement bears its natural fruit in untroubledness of soul, the highest well-being humans are capable of.

Yes, it is now clear that the ancient doctrine was from the beginning moving, only half awarely, in the same direction as this new thinking. To believe that serenity can be achieved by eschewing dogmatism in matters of knowledge is to make no *theoretical* claim whatsoever; it simply abandons the sovereign demands of theory. It was, however, as can be seen now, perhaps somewhat too subjective. Suspension of judgement and serenity were thought of too much as states of mind, whereas they can be taken to say equally much about the nature of things. In suspending judgement one discovers that things bring no judgement with them, and the serene mind discovers that things are serene in themselves. In contrast, the gnoseal enterprise is impatient; it measures things in terms of its own purposes and calculations. It is not receptive, it does not give things leave to speak in their own voices. Human well-being, however, is living with things, inner and outer, in such freedom that their worth can grow into the human world and enrich it beyond the wisest calculations. The best way of being with things is *not* to transfix them with the arrows of knowledge. This I now see to be a clear principle.

There is, of course, an unavoidable and just objection to this. To speak so confidently of suspension of judgement and serenity is to ignore the dictum "Names do not name." It appears to be one more gnoseal dogmatism, this time of a behavioural kind. The key terms being used must be making just as clear a claim to knowledge as the key terms in all theories. "Suspension of judgement" and "serenity" attempt to fix, by naming, certain acts and states. But if names do not name then they are as illegitimate and as useless as any other preferred vocabulary.

This seems fair in a traditional way and yet it misses the new point being made. The terms "suspension of judgement" and "serenity" appear to function gnoseally, but do not really. "Words serve primarily to evoke and guide behaviour" was perhaps the most radical, the most seminal thought of Nagaraj's remarkable barrage of ideas. Initial difficulties in applying this dictum to all theories – physical, metaphysical and theological – about the structure of the world will be great and the indignation aroused will be vehement. But it should be easier in the case of a teaching like my own which counsels a certain *way* of coming to terms with the nature of things, of coping with the behaviour of the world itself. "Middle way," "the great tao," "untroubledness of soul" are not structural descriptions, but unmistakable challenges and encouragements to a vivial stance, a life attitude.

These words evoke appropriate responses and somehow guide toward the realization of their own sense. This effect will be exactly what was intended by the dictum "Words evoke and guide behaviour." Now if words can guide behaviour there must be some tolerably reliable bond joining the initial use of a word to the outcome it is intended to lead to. If one encourages to serenity of mind it can't be that frenetic restlessness will ensue as probably as calm good humour. Words must carry their incipient realization in themselves; they must bring their own ductal sense with them. They fulfil themselves, to put it so, within the universe of the language being used. The new thought must be that they do this not through naming a state of affairs that exists whether named or no, but by fulfilling themselves in the aware behaviour to which they lead. Ludwig ventured very close to this thought when he said, "Our behaviour gives the full meaning to our words."

There have been those who centred their thinking around the ancient word *pragma* – act, thing – from my own language. They were enthused by the experimental sciences of their day and gave a heavy preference to concrete facts and individual behaviour toward them. Any belief or theory which furthered fruitful commerce with the concrete qualified as truth. The prominence of behaviour in their thinking is sympathetic to myself and would be to Nagaraj, if he knew about them. But the *pragma* thinkers treated behaviour more as the medium in which ideas are tested for their truth, whereas Nagaraj is telling us that ideas realize their sense *as*, and metamorphose *into* aware behaviour. I am sure he would find the pragmatic focus on finite, everyday situations as the matrix of truth too fragmented and laden with unexamined presumptions. Against that he trusted in the self-disciplining pursuit of vivial sense to range unhindered in and out of behaviour and ideas. A separation of behaviour and sense is not intelligible. Still, the *pragma* thinkers would have had an initial access to "ideas fulfilling themselves." How freely philosophies appear in different ages.

Most men, however, will find initial access difficult. "Ideas fulfilling themselves" will strike men commonly as unconvincing or even as lacking in sense. A phrase "suspension of judgement" is supposed to acquire its meaning by issuing into, fulfilling itself in, another behavioural phrase, "untroubledness of soul." How can it be that a verbal expression, "suspension of judgement," which by our own wish has no definable meaning, can fulfil itself in another expression of no definable meaning, "untroubledness of soul," especially when the word that joins them, "fulfilment," which is supposed to explain how words can evoke and guide, has itself no determinable meaning? This is unintelligible. How can words "evoke and guide behaviour" if a name does not designate one kind of behaviour rather than another? How will it be possible to be sure if and when a word that names nothing has fulfilled itself in another word that names nothing? How can there be any sense at all left in words if there is not only nothing for them to name, but if, as must follow, the word "naming" itself names nothing. This new train of thought becomes unintelligible because we can't say what it is we are trying to say.

Does this not loose the very notion of language having sense into the outer spaces of sceptical nihilism?

Will it not appear that the human scene has disintegrated into a mass of meaningless words and acts from which there is no escape, a zoo of gibbering idiots? Will this tortuous sceptical tour not appear to have been a disaster, miring men more deeply in despair than before? Will this be the end of scepticism, the bitter fruit of questioning the sanctity of knowledge? Should we not turn back and uproot the entire sceptical enterprise? Was Aristos' warning prophetic?

Men will entertain such misgivings – there can be no doubt about that – and they cannot be brushed aside. We will have to show up the misconception on which they rest. We have all become comfortable within the familiar belief that ideas are primarily cognitive devices. We feel insecure and disoriented if this dogma is disrupted and we must survive outside its protection. Nagaraj insisted that the gnoseal dogma is delusion and tried to show this. But we must now recognize the puzzlements thrown up by this exposure and try to show in what ways ideas and words and behaviour and thought and belief can make sense after the spell of the dogma of knowledge has been shattered.

There will have to be a fresh beginning, a reaching behind and underneath the most ancient of men's beliefs about themselves and their world, beliefs which are the anchor of philosophy. The sundering of all things into an unchanging world, external to human purposes, on the one hand, and an inner world of feelings, ideas and language, somehow dependent on an individual consciousness, on the other, hobbles spontaneous thought and behaviour. This impeccable dichotomy, this cleavage of the vivial realm has strengthened some religions and is a presupposition of our physical sciences, but it distorts the world in which human destinies are woven, the world where philosophies are born and serve their purpose. For the very ribcage and breathing spirit of this human world is that it not be external to human purposes but responsive to them. Within the reach of human behaviour, inner and external worlds are reciprocally permeable in one world of vivial sense.

We will have to see that "inner" and "outer" are not self-contained realms, each repudiating the other yet yoked together unintelligibly, as they have been in so much of our philosophy. They remain of course ineluctable structures of the everyday; they orient primally. Yet named-things, which are commonly thought to be at home in the outer world, penetrate the inner world easily because of their being named. Name has inner access by birthright. Named ideas and named feelings, which are commonly thought to be at home in the inner world, are in their turn unintelligible if separated from the outer hemisphere in conjunction with which they arise and where they find their natural fulfilment. Ideas and feelings, being susceptible to naming, can, in their own way, be taken as entities. This is clearer now since Nagaraj spoke and it explains why he faulted my earlier distinction between the thing honey and the taste of honey: both, being named, are, in his sense, entities.

Inner ideas and feelings and outer things move easily in and out of each other's supposed exclusive realm as if there were no boundary between them. The globular cinder circling the earth, when seen glowing with the sun's light through dark nights, when experienced as a kindly, silent companion by the love-struck, when known as the measure of time, becomes, *in the act of saying the word "moon,"* the moon. The moon is not merely a thing in space, it is an eloquent part of the inner world of poetic feelings and religious reverence. In the same way, reversed, a named idea-feeling, or felt-idea, "courage" would be an example, becomes an element in the outer, social world. A certain inner strength, obstinacy and generosity in one, magically become "courage" when value sensitivity gives birth to the name-idea "courage," but not before. Once named, courage is recognizable in the behaviour of others as well as in oneself and becomes a stable element in the social world.

So the apparently simple act of naming will be understood in a new way. It becomes the mysterious process or at least the visible aspect of it, by which men *form* the world within and around them. Whatever is of importance comes to be named. The unnamed is over the horizon or under the surface and can assume a place in the ordered world only as it is transformed by a name. The name and what is named are not two and separate, neither as name and idea nor as name and thing. The world is not like an array of bottles at a wine tasting, each with its specific contents, patiently waiting for men to paste the correct labels on them. Language and things are not indifferent to each other in that way. Name and what is named will be seen to be interdependent if Nagaraj's thinking is followed up; neither can have existence or be intelligible without the other. Names and things – odd, even alienating, as this sounds – arise together in the one creative act. They are but two aspects of one act and cannot in good sense be kept apart. There is no moon without the concept "moon"; there is no courage without the concept "courage"; there is no war without the concept "war"; and no peace without the concept "peace". So it is that things and events of the "outer" world come to meet men already tamed and assimilable to human understanding and purposes. And so the ideas and feelings of the "inner" world, insofar as named, are amenable to exchange and transaction in the social order.

This understanding replaces a commonly-held view of meaning. Ideas need no longer be seen as free-floating meanings, inner epistemic objects which must be true or false if predicated of states of affairs independent of them. The new thought is that ideas are already imbedded in the structure of the world, inner and outer, that comes to meet us. Meaning can, of course, be set over against neutral states of affairs if we lift the transactions of knowing out of their total vivial setting. Within the abstracted structure of those transactions it will continue to make sense to speak of meaning in opposition to what meaning is predicated of. When ideas, names and things are restored to their full vivial habitat, however, it becomes clear that only in their interdependence are they the flesh and blood and bones of the human scene, inner and outer. Meaning, though gnoseally it appears to be quite separate from the things of which it is the meaning, is, vivially, a nucleus of remembered and anticipated experience, the substance of named-things. As the fusion of inner and outer, the object-as-understood, meaning affords freedom to adjust and manoeuvre toward the future. It makes human behaviour possible. Its function should be seen within the full frame of the human scene. Its specialized function within the knowing situation should not henceforth be taken as its sole or proper definition.

I wondered earlier if the dictum "names do not name" might be the final grave and resting place of scepticism. It appeared probable that most men would think it was that. If, however, name and what is named arise together, if meanings and theories are not separated from the objects and structures of the public scene as "inner" and "outer" suggest, are not inhabitants of a private world, then the traditional understanding of knowledge as the essential bond between a human and the world, as the pivotal fact of existence, can be repudiated with good sense. Nagaraj's dictum becomes, not an avowal of nihilism, but a pointer at the spontaneous and living character of the world, at its essentially human character. "Names do not name" may be an act of liberation long awaited.

The traditional opposition between theory and practice now appears faulty and a way is suggested for superseding it. Ideas can be seen, not as virginal meanings which must be married to the harshness of things through action, but as themselves nothing less than incipient action. Ideas do in fact move us, sometimes to further thought, sometimes to overt action, but always and by their nature they are the seeds of behaviour. Thinking itself can be seen as its own kind of behaviour. Ideas unfold in ways of behaving, in the speech of action. Action, in its turn, feeds new sense into ideas and tests their worth. Ideas and action live as one in the aware act. Ideas fulfilling themselves – the course of aware behaviour – is a magical cycle. It is the process of thought absorbing the nature of things into itself and so growing; and of things revealing themselves in the constraints they put on action; which in its turn re-shapes thought. Learning and teaching exemplify this cycle simply.

Aware behaviour is neither merely gnoseal nor merely behavioural, these being abstractions for special purposes. On being urged, for example, to be "courageous," one begins with the name-idea "courage" and moves in the direction it suggests. There is no definition to be followed, no norm to be met, only a protean value sense probing forward. On the way one will discover much about oneself and about the alchemy of the human spirit, and this will result in refining and deepening the initial idea. "Courage" will be whatever such an aware fulfilment brings with it. If its pursuit results in a breakdown of the social situation for whose sake courage was urged, then it will be clear that the idea was wrongly seized initially: what fulfilled itself was not courage but, perhaps, staged heroism or self-will. The fulfilment of the idea cannot be capricious. It will be either self-validating or self-nullifying in some degree. There can be no final clarity, and so the exploration goes on. This can perhaps be thought of and accepted as *truthing*, even though there is no truth.

All this has come of marrying my old doctrines of the suspension of judgement and serenity of mind to the new dicta: "Truth is not the concern of knowledge but of vivial discipline" and "Knowing things is not the best way of being with things." I am carried forward. Would that I could hold back, but I cannot. Nagaraj's ideas seem a natural completion of my own.

He has allowed us to see what exciting possibilities for understanding the human scene open up after knowledge has been dethroned in favour of the search for life-sense. This search moves as aware behaviour into the furthest reaches of philosophy and science. We have not before conceived these as aware behaviour, as idea-fulfilment, but now we can. The great three-fold *Aufhebung,* the idealism of *eidos* and copy, Aristos' own search for the highest causes, are all equally expressions of a life-sense. Being philosophies they naturally have the form of theories. But as life-sense they take their place alongside enlightenment and the tao in a larger family. This is an assault on the enabling presumption of philosophy – truth as theoretical knowledge – and frees it from the epistemic thrall.

This is as far as I, a sceptic, can allow my thinking to go. No comfort of truth is offered in the course of radical scepsis. The new vocabulary – "aware behaviour," "idea fulfilment," "truthing" – can make no more claim to truth than the old vocabulary – "knowledge," "reality," "truth" – did. It functions in exactly the same evocative and guiding way as all idea-words do. Now, however, it has become possible to acknowledge this frankly and to face its possibilities – and these will cut deep and hurt in the cutting.

At this turn the words of Nagaraj and the echoes of the afternoon completed their soliloqual round of the doubting brothers and became still in the thinking of each of them singly.

Evening
The Magic of Unknowing

The Common Brooding

The sons of Aristos of Gnosis looked at each other around their family circle, not sure where their thinking would take them now. An evening breeze drifted silently up from the lake and the great tree murmured quietly to itself as if still brooding on the passage of the storm. Somehow, though it could not be said how, the puzzlements and disclosures of the day continued to gestate in the common mind of the family of brothers, and in the common brooding much became clearer.

* * * * * *

Scepsis has run its full course and so have our philosophic efforts to resolve it. Gnoseal delusion was announced and awareness of it has arrived. But the puzzlement reaches deeper than academic scepticism. It is not merely a question of critically re-valuing the traditional philosophic faith in the power of knowledge. Men may well be able to survive without this faith; but will they be able to survive without some other certainty to take its place? And how can there be some new certainty, if the notion of certainty is as indefinable as all notions, which is to say, if certainty cannot be taken to mean what men have always thought it meant? Certainty brings no certainty of its own meaning, so it will not be possible, in good sense, to be certain of anything, whether of knowledge, of value, of belief. We will no longer be able to say "I may not *know* the truth but I am at least certain what I *believe,* what my own certainties *are*." We will no longer be able, in honesty, to say even that.

It now seems that we are not only gnoseally but also vivially adrift; we are in the end incapable of *knowing* anything, as the sceptics insist, but are also, even more disturbingly, unable to be *sure* of anything, not of right and wrong, of good and bad or even of what is inner and what is outer. The new vocabulary, "aware behaviour" and "idea fulfilment," offered to us this afternoon to replace the language of knowledge, served only to open up to us the depths of the vivial drift, for it did nothing to offer any kind of vivial certainty in place of the gnoseal certainty it elbowed aside. The comforting belief in knowledge and science was, if limited, at least an effective practical belief; it was itself a kind of vivial certainty. Now there is nothing, not even certainty about what "certainty" means. That no one will be able to be sure what his convictions mean – whether one holds that human well-being lies in wisdom, or in enlightenment or in the tao – follows from the gnoseal blindness of all such words.

If this is now seized on in its relentless pervasiveness it becomes clear that men's most basic and enabling beliefs, the beliefs which, together, form the very possibility of everyday life, are as bereft of solid ground as the special beliefs of morals and religion are. Each human lives by the belief that deep inside the wrappings and disguises of habit and convention there is his real self; that the everyday world of objects is external to and independent of himself but given in the certainty of knowledge; that through decisions reached in the freedom of privacy, he intervenes autocratically in the events of his world. Each human lives by such beliefs even though, as the work of the afternoon showed, they are quite unintelligible. Yet they are needed if men are to remain alive in the world.

This is a new turning point, forced on us by our work this day. It is no longer gnoseal delusion, no longer the unintelligibility of metaphysical or scientific theories. This turn shows up the paradox knotted into the core of human existence: life is possible only on the back of a cluster of beliefs which must be held to be untrue. This is a kind of civil strife, the intellect warring with its brother faculties. It is not just that there is some measure of unclarity or uncertainty or even contradiction in our beliefs; it is that in order to survive men must believe what they must hold to be untrue. Demonstrating, even arguing for the untruth of a belief – let it be, for an example, belief in an inner self as the agent person, as was so vigorously attempted earlier this afternoon – is possible only by acting out its truth. To demonstrate or argue that the agent person is an unintelligible notion is possible only if the one arguing acts as if both he and those he is arguing with *are* agent persons. To argue the untruth of such beliefs reinforces their truth and yet the impossibility of their truth is being demonstrated. Our subtlest insights are contradicted in the act of their pronouncement. This paradox is more than puzzlement. It is stupefying, it is the most telling character of human life, the mud bath in which men try to wash their clods of earth. It recalls the idea-words "dream" and "magic" from the stormy pronouncement, "The everyday world is a dream, a magic show."

So far buddhist and Sanskrit thinking penetrated this afternoon. It was clear that the absurdities of the everyday had no power to stifle buddhist or other sanscritic faith. For them, pronouncing the everyday a dream and a magic show transparences absurdities and opens a way into the world of enlightenment. For those not of this faith "dream" and "magic show" become not a final resolution, but a challenge to the hardest thinking. They must be tested for their vivial worth as evocative and guiding notions.

"Dream," "magic," these unphilosophical terms, though they arise naturally at this point, of course explain nothing. As the sole nameable issue of the day's work they are surely more than mere figures of speech, yet metaphors they are nonetheless. As such they remind us that we have failed to find sure ground for our thinking, or bedrock for our living. Though they may lift the heart and excite the imagination, they do nothing to counter the toxic effects of scepticism and vivial drift. Most men will wonder if "dream" and "magic" are not feebler and more vacuous than the earlier terms "belief," "knowledge," and "truth." They will wonder if this thinking is not progressing downhill, if the embrace of meaninglessness is not tightening around them. Now, so it will appear, there is nothing left to men even of ethical value. A universal moral law or a vision of the new trans-human being will no longer have the power to arouse belief or secure dignity to human life. Men will think themselves thrown into the winds of time and fortune helplessly. They will think it better to retain their conventional beliefs even without the prestigious patina of knowledge. Scepsis will be seen to have uselessly undermined everything and, in the end, to have made a farce of itself. The only thing beyond doubt, men will be sure to think, is that doubt has achieved nothing.

So it may seem. So it will seem to most. But our cogitations of this afternoon, the attacks on our common beliefs, could not have been farce, or meaningless. They were not capricious polemics, for each attack on the sanctity of philosophy arose from an inherent feebleness in the defence offered by its predecessors. It was as if each earnest pronouncement rode on the back of a deeply buried, implicit belief in an alternative to philosophy stronger than the philosophic beliefs it demolished.

How could we have agreed, even if reluctantly, that the great doctrines of our philosophical tradition could be impotenced or transparenced if there were no common, even though unrecognized, depth from which the sceptical thrusts were echoing back? Each of our great doctrines in turn opened its hands to show them empty of gnoseal certainty when scepsis forced the issue: "I think therefore I am," "I can know *that* I am but not *what* I am," "A creative force returns eternally in all things," "Belief must take the place of knowledge," "There is no escape from language to nature." Each of these doctrines was felled, and torn from its cognitive roots. Each reached in behind its predecessors to whatever it found there that required and justified their repudiation. Yet this transparencing, it was clear, should not be mistaken for a dialectical *Aufhebung*.

But how are we to grasp this? Each sceptical probe, in the end, was not able to say, did not want to say, what it had discovered that invalidated the doctrine under attack except, of course, that it had proved devoid of intelligibility. Some common acceptance of this, even if inexplicit, must have carried the long, winding exploration of the afternoon. It would be hard to grasp the persuasive trajectory of this experience without supposing a common *source* of confidence in the process of transparencing metaphysical doctrines, of holding them up to view minus their cognitive roots. A common scepsis cannot be vagrant or irresponsible. It suggests, perhaps requires, the supposition of a sub-surface guidance for its fumblings and gropings. Scepsis allows us to be sure that metaphysical doctrines defy validation as true or false, but, more than that and incisively, it allows us to be sure that the source of this confidence is no definable idea or name-word. It is not a term in a new metaphysics.

This source awareness, which carries and guides root scepsis, cannot be a privileged sense reserved for philosophers; we must be able to observe its workings in the everyday as well. Life for most of us is a stumbling over and a futile groping for the meaning of a loose network of prestigious ideas, our primitive metaphysics or complex of superstitions. Men live in adventure with idea-words like "science," "person," "future," "technology," and yet are quite unable to give a clear account of their meaning or worth. On being approached closely each and every term evades us. This can easily appear to be the black food of nihilism. But it can also be seen as the matrix out of which can issue the merits and the magic of scepticism. The stumbling over and fumbling with ideas is not a natural event like a rainstorm, but appears to be carried forward by a slumbering awareness that behind every repudiated idea there must be, not *reasons* for the repudiation, but some dumb sense of the idea's inadequacy. Scepsis does not stagger capriciously among prestigious ideas, but moves through the facade of one to the seeming substance of another, and then through that to another, more embracingly. In the everyday this dumb sense is buried deep, but to presume its working there is as compelling as it is to presume it among philosophers.

It is gradually becoming clear to us that everything turns on this dumb sense, or source awareness. We can recognize it in the way it voices its presence without using names. It comes to us as uncaused, spontaneous. It is not idea, not part of any system of ideas, nor has it meaning. It brings its own light with it, so to speak. It appears to enter on the scene of vivial exploration simply as itself, though we cannot *say* what that is. Though not word or idea, it bears these up with whatever sense they aspire to. It gives itself effortlessly as the source of meaning without itself having any nameable meaning. Against its dumb wisdom all ideas and all doctrines – philosophical, taoist, buddhist, scientific – appear hollow, groundless, failures, a mummery of their own pretensions. If approached for usable, verbal meaning it frustrates with its silence, and is henceforth unmistakable. Once the source is discovered, the everyday world of be-named realities, inner and outer, rises up in the starkest contrast, loses its substance and becomes a world of shapes and surfaces and names, and no more.

This dumb sense of source, we are coming to see,

and nothing else, can awaken men to realize that they live in a world of greater frame than the be-worded everyday. It tells them of a source that does not reside among worded realities as one more worded reality, however transcendental or divine. Not being a what, neither a god nor Being itself, it can only transparence worded realities – from carpenters' tools to ancient texts – and reveal the truths behind their names. Yet it cannot itself tell men in men's words how this transparencing is to be enacted. This awakening tells them that, in listening to the source, they are discovering themselves. "I think therefore I am" came close to this; it transparenced everything save the names, "thinking", "I" and "am", but stopped short there. The afternoon's work made it clear that even the immediacy of thinking cannot be the resting place of scepsis. It too, under further probing, was loosened from the source of its meaning, concealed behind the idea-words "thinking", "I" and "am", and so was transparenced.

This unworded source of worded ideas and worded things is, as we have come to see, the last, and the first, and the only, hope for vivial sense in a world made up of worded ideas and worded things all claiming in magical delusion to be real *in their own right as named.* The self-fulfilment of ideas in aware behaviour is not a matter of blind stumbling and groping through clouds of disputation. It is the one measure of sense available to men. It can be understood only as being guided from within by silent promptings from the source awareness or, when an idea is failing to fulfil itself, by silent warnings. The fulfilment of ideas which have no definable meaning is, in good sense, possible only because of the transparencing of the ideas and things which form the scene of the action. Living without the comfort of belief in knowledge, or any other dogma, is possible because ideas fulfilling themselves, aware behaviour, is not random, which would be madness, but moves cheek by jowl with the silent source of sense.

All this can, and very likely will, give rise to a great misconception. Men will be tempted to understand themselves as inhabitants of two realms: the word-effective everyday and the unworded, transparencing awareness of it. The simple fact that men can become aware of the be-worded and be-thinged world *as* an enclosure may be taken as evidence that they inhabit a world beyond it. The idealistic thought of two worlds – the natural order of science and the suprasensible order of morals and religion – which was presented so eloquently earlier this afternoon came close to suggesting this. To separate source and everyday in this ontic sense, however, violates each in itself and both in their symbiosis. Source is source only *of* the everyday. It is, so far as humans will ever be sure, nothing apart from that. To give it an ontic status as a realm additional to the everyday would be to misunderstand wholly. It is better to think that men are capable of two *ways* of seeing and taking things and people and themselves. It is better to think that, in their proud assertion of self-worth – reality – people and things of the everyday lose their lustre and worth; that openness to the source can let this lustre and worth back in. These would be two ways of being with people and things in the *one* world.

This is, nonetheless, a crippled endowment, and eerie. It would have us believe that man is capable of becoming aware of what *fails* to be true, but is unable to say what *is* true. He is permitted, apparently, only a hint of the power denied him. He is fated to be lured only by a dream of what it might be to know a truth. This makes man a haunted being – sure, even before he speaks and even as he speaks, that everything he will say must be false. This makes man the one who must discover that he cannot *know* what it is that he is sure of; that nothing is what his most clarified understanding tells him it is; that he cannot at any time *know* what he is feeling or thinking or doing. This makes man the one who must discover not merely that man's truths are untrue but that man's sense of truth is false: he must believe what he has no grounds for holding to be true. This makes man the one who must discover that the mighty world of the everyday is a magic enclosure from which there is no escape; *and* the one to discover that this great heaving ocean of worded falsity is yet the only entrance vouchsafed men to the unworded source which declares it false.

To discover this, the simple conclusion of a little reflection, will it not, once again, evoke the words "dream" and "magic," but this time as if one were *in* the dream and *part of* the magic?

Can our brooding rest here? Of all the doctrinal idea-words which have been offered and tested and repudiated this day – "truth," "tao," "enlightenment," "knowledge" – "dream" and "magic" have been the most stubborn, the longest-lived. As hapless descriptions, as metaphysical surrogates they have already been repudiated; they are as incapable of ceasing to be language as any other preferred terms. But if they are taken in their vivial sense, as evocative, hortatory, ductal words, is there not much to be said for them? "Dream," "magic," as named – ideas, are their own explosive, sustaining propulsion. They are capable of releasing a swarm of age-old repressions, of allowing spontaneity into thought and feeling, of giving a new reach and depth to our life-sense. They will, no doubt, arouse their own fear at the abyssal character of life, its want of bedrock; but they can arouse a new courage to accept the adventural and wholly bewildering nature of existence. Most humans are victims of this bewilderment in any case, though they seldom speak about it, commonly leaving their dis-ease to fester beneath the surface.

Though "dream" and "magic" must remain indefinable, they will be quite useless, even harmful, if left to drift without a nisal thrust. The purposes to which these words may be turned require understanding. Will it be just the be-worded everyday world, the capsule of delusion in which humans pass most of their lives, that is the dream and the magic show? It has often been so described by those who say they have awakened from it. Yet, if only the everyday is dream-like and magical, then the source awareness, which announces itself as beyond the everyday, will remain outside the dream and the magic show as a bedrock reality. This would be to re-state the ancient claim of the mystics and prophets, Buddha and the others, to a singular access to knowledge. In such case it would not be the whole of human existence which merited the dream or magic word, but only a part of it. This would be quite unacceptable, amounting to a new and sterile dogmatism, less rational than the old metaphysics and less powerful than the old religions. It would denigrate common life in favour of an incorrigible, revelatory inner voice which was impotent to reveal anything.

Again "dream" and "magic show" may be thought of as applying to the awakening from the everyday itself. *That* the human can become aware of himself as the inhabitant of a world which he repudiates, as it were the unwilling yet unresisting victim of an enthralment, is this the dream and the magic? *That* he can become aware of himself as belonging to a world beyond the world he repudiates, yet helpless against his natural membership in the repudiated world, is this the dream and the magic? Is it this sense of being condemned to an enthralment he has not chosen, whilst glimpsing his freedom in a truth withheld from him, which arouses the sense of dream and magic show? This would be more adequate than limiting dream and magic to the everyday alone.

Still, it leaves the significance of the source awareness itself in some doubt. Is it or is it not to be taken as within the dream, as part of the magic show? The source awareness is inseparable from the everyday. That much has become clear from the way it enters the scene: it appears only *as* the awakening from and the transparencing of the worded things of the everyday. We can note it in no other way. It will, in this sense, have to be within the dream and the magic show. Yet, if it is, it will become as dream-like as the falsities of the everyday, which is to say it will cease to be what it is and the despair of nihilism will be loose again. This is not acceptable sense for, as we have learned, the source awareness emerges on the human scene as the one and only element there which is *self*-announced, and is not given in a network of idea-words. It functions as a true source, spontaneous and underived, a touchstone for all else. It cannot be of the same dream stuff as the everyday.

So the source, the non-thinged awareness, it might appear, is *both* within and not within the dream and the magic show. As both possibilities have been seen to be unintelligible in themselves, it would be better to turn that notion around and say that the source awareness is *neither* wholly within the everyday *nor* wholly without, If it were within the everyday it could not be the source of awakening from it. If it were without it would invoke some causal notion and lose its indissoluble symbiosis with the everyday, the only way of being its source. "Neither-nor" is clearly no more intelligible in itself than "both," yet better because it asserts less and because it allows the awareness of words and things without the use of words – what we have found we must accept – to make more sense of the magic of human existence. "Within," "without" – to expect such idea-words to function epistemically, however much they help in other ways, is to perpetuate the gnoseal delusion.

We have come to a climactic point. The terms "delusory everyday" and "source," now indispensable to our exploration, remain as unintelligible as all pairs of concepts necessarily always are. Each of the pair must presuppose the other before it can begin to have a meaning of its own, and so each nullifies itself and its partner. That both say more than they have any right to and yet less than they claim to, is itself the most striking experience of magic possible. Without them we must abandon the attempt to explore for life-sense, with them we are lured into further delusion. At that point in their reach for truth where humans want most desperately to be sure, they are mocked by the futility of their ambition. Is it so that men in the present age will have to be content to say that the awakening from the dream of the everyday is not an awakening into a non-dream world of irrefragable truths – as all religions and philosophies pronounce – but, in some puzzling way, into a different, let it be a "higher", dream . . . yet still a dream?

Can this in any way ease the last confrontation between delusion and certainty?

The source seems to hint at the possibility of, even to offer the promise of a reality, a truth, a life beyond the everyday. This hint, this promise will of course be mistaken, by those searching for a truth beyond science and common reason, as unarguable confirmation of whatever their philosophy or religion happens to be. They will believe they have discovered an entrance into a world of suprahuman powers.

We must be on our guard at this point. No new possibilities of gnoseal answers have opened up. In the voice and wisdom of the source there is as little *knowledge* as there was in the everyday dream. Even the most careful exploration of the source, if it is understood as Being, over-reaches our powers. Being and knowing are too closely twinned to be separated by the effort of thinking: if we cannot know we cannot assert Being. Unless it can be taken in a ductal, vivial sense, Being wrongly imposes its form on the source.

We must see clearly that "source" is not a name for an existent something. Its elusiveness is not a sign of higher existence. "Source" is offered only to arouse a sense of direction in which vivial exploration may go. It suggests a way of taking, of behaving toward, of understanding what appears to appear at the culmination of our attempt to explore under and behind the everyday world. It is essential to the special life-sense emerging for us this afternoon, but it is not metaphysics.

It might be said that what, in the everyday, was dogma or enthralment – knowledge or enlightenment or the tao as the key to human existence – in the source as higher dream becomes the faintest hope that just conceivably there might be, somewhere, a self-luminous, self-transparencing truth, even if not ever available to humans *as* that. But this is of course inadmissable, truth being, strictly, a term of the everyday. Men commonly talk about their deepest need in terms of truth. The higher dream, which the source brings us, seems to hold out the promise that our profoundest everyday truths can be true in the higher sense. But it is only a promise, and can never be kept. Yet, though often thus falsely grasped, it cannot be denied; it is the one promise which can never be withdrawn.

If the scepsis of this long day has led us anywhere it is to see that "dream" and "magic" are not names and do not define any aspect of life. These idea-words, the last to survive the acid of scepsis, are, like all their fellows, evocative and ductal, not designatory. "Higher dream" and "source awareness" are not dogmatic certainties. They cannot be claimed as knowledge or as evidence for enlightenment or the tao. Yet they are not fantasy-made fictions either. Their meaning lies in the experiences and life they lead to, in the aware behaviour of their dreamlike, their magical fulfilment. We can escape some confusion at this ending if we see that "truthing" – an idea fulfilling itself vivially, not merely gnoseally – includes truth in the sense of the "higher dream." The new orientation is coming to see all vivial absolutes as unacknowledged pre-emptions of the "higher dream." They are surrogates which, driven to their last gasp, can transparence into vivial truthing.

The idea-words "dream," "magic," and "source" claim preference to "knowledge," "reality," and "truth" in that, unlike these, they do not fail to fulfil themselves when put to the vivial test. Whereas "knowledge," "reality," and "truth" abandon the thinker at the very point where their promise should be kept, dissipating themselves in their failed fulfilment, "dream," "magic," and "truthing" evoke expectations which can be fulfilled. The more one is open to the fullness of vivial exploration, to the many wondrous ways of making sense, the more these ideas grow in strength.

So, for the present, the resting place of this winding exploration – the issue of our day's hard thinking – is simply the thought that life ceases to bewilder as dream and magic show when one lives these ideas to their fulfilment. So it can then be said, paradoxically, that human existence makes best sense as the not-sense of magic and dream.

* * * * * *

The common brooding of all the brothers came to rest, exhausted. It held its breath for a long moment as if waiting for a sign of release.

Then, no one could say from where, a final pulse moved their thinking on to the conclusion of its labours.

* * * * * *

We have lived through the irreversible erosion of the philosophic faith in the past centuries. We have survived the assault on it from without in our own time. We have rescued what we honourably could for ourselves and our descendants.

Scepsis pushed us into the abyss of unknowing where we found traces leading to the source, and the goal, of our explorations. We saw that all life-truths held as dogmas, and not only philosophy's faith in knowledge,are without ground in reason. They are like spells or enthralments descended from nowhere to inspire us with accounts of human destiny that we receive as good sense. It now becomes decisive to see that the life-truths of the tao and of enlightenment, worthy to stand beside philosophy's faith in knowledge, are, in the same way and degree, misappropriations of the dream-truth promised by the source. Great as all these truth-dogmas have been, in our time they must be held up to the harsh light of scepsis as we have tried to do. If we fail to do this, the truth-dogmas of past classical ages will constrict and enfeeble vivial exploration for our time and in the future. Already the great enthralment to knowledge is becoming an obsession with technical data, and enlightenment has become merely an altered state of consciousness.

If this thought holds, and our family council of this afternoon lends some substance to it, we can already see our sceptical exploration embracing wider concerns. Scepsis will trace in the horizons of the possibility of all vivial exploration in our time. That unaware presumptions – enthralments we are calling them – not reason, should have emerged in our time as the unacknowledged power and authority of all classical dogmas, lays a special privilege and obligation on us. We can approach all traditions with one question uppermost. We can enquire what presumptions lie buried in their insights and arguments. We can enquire what it is that allows their conclusions to appear self-evidently relevant and sensible. We can trace the thinking in each case back to its genetive scope: its way of grasping what the source was trying to say to it. From this pursuit we can learn more about the human quest for vivial sense than from any other kind of study. It will enable us to compare the enthralments of the different traditions with a view to grasping more clearly how hidden enthralments inspire vivial exploration. What a privilege: to be humble participants in the unearthing of great hidden thoughts from the past, to be alive in this time of transition to a radically new era of vivial exploration.

Scepsis brings its obligation as well. We are no longer free to pretend that even our most critical sense of the character of human destiny is a truth. We have seen that of its own nature the source must deceive us. It appears as truth or being and the unwary take it as that. But it is a promise only, a promise never withdrawn, but never kept. We vivial sceptics recognize it as a dream-truth. It lures us with the hope that somewhere, in some way, in or out of time, there is a true truth, but it does no more than that. The obligation of the sceptical is not to forget this, not to accept would-be dogma-truths. There is no other way to hold open access to the source for future times, and it is not written in the stars that the source will always be accessible.

What a privilege, and what an obligation! Who can say whether one day new and great enthralments will not inspire men's thinking again. That must be our best hope. It is more conceivable the more the common mind of our time remains free of constricting superstitions. The more men understand how easily they can mistake a glimpse of the source for an eternal truth, the less likely it is that debilitating enthralments – perhaps "information" and "mind-states" – will determine men's life-sense in the future. The classical no longer hold us in thrall; they have surfaced and lost their power. The best hope we can have for the future is that the source will remain accessible to us. If it does, seeming-truths will have a short life and the happy day may dawn when powerful enthralments can form again, enthralments as universal and life-giving as the ancient thralls of knowledge, the tao and enlightenment.

Until then, vivial scepsis will be our front line of defence.

* * * * * *

The fraternal, arboreal brooding rested. A sense of completion, if only for the day, pervaded the family circle. The brothers stirred and awoke from their labours. The common brooding on the magical consequences of scepsis came finally and peacefully to rest.

The disappearing sun threw its farewell light on the ancient mansion of Aristos of Gnosis as his sceptical sons, foster and natural, the oldest from Elis, René, Immanuel, David, Friedrich, Ludwig, Chang and Nagaraj rested in repose under the great maple, their bodies speaking the labour they had been through, their faces the calm of the evening which had followed the storm.

Looking down on the circle of great men below, the tree thought, "There are more bonds between the everyday and its source than scepsis. But for now it is enough if they are able to live out what they have discovered this day."

Author's Note

Readers not closely acquainted with Western philosophy and Eastern thought may not at once recognize the characters in this soliloquy as the namesakes of historical persons, thus: Aristos (Aristotle), René (Descartes), Immanuel (Kant), David (Hume), Friedrich (Nietzsche), Ludwig (Wittgenstein), the brother from Elis (Pyrrho), Chang (Chuang Tzu) and Nagaraj (Nagarjuna).

In the first encounter of the soliloquy – *Erosion from Within* – each of the imaginary characters advances views which his historical namesake would, the author believes, accept as his own, though of course these views are selected and expressed so as to develop the theme of the soliloquy.

Following the *Storm* each of the Western characters, by and for himself, re-thinks his philosophy under pressure of the challenge from the East. The account given of this re-thinking – *Metamorphosis* – is the author's conception of the way Western philosophers might have opened their thinking to the ideas of Nagarjuna and Chuang Tzu.

The issue of this imagined metamorphosis – life as dream and magic – is given in the *Common Brooding* and is the author's reach into the future.

Those for whom Chuang Tzu and Nagarjuna are strange names may like to have these titles:

Chuang Tzu by Burton Watson
Lucid Exposition of the Middle Way: Essential Chapters from the Prasannapada, translated from the Sanscrit by Mervyn Sprung

About the Publisher

The word "broadview" expresses a good deal of the philosophy behind our company. Our focus is very much on the humanities and social sciences—especially literature, writing, and philosophy—but within these fields we are open to a broad range of academic approaches and political viewpoints. We strive in particular to produce high-quality, pedagogically useful books for higher education classrooms—anthologies, editions, sourcebooks, surveys of particular academic fields and sub-fields, and also course texts for subjects such as composition, business communication, and critical thinking. We welcome the perspectives of authors from marginalized and underrepresented groups, and we have a strong commitment to the environment. We publish English-language works and translations from many parts of the world, and our books are available world-wide; we also publish a select list of titles with a specifically Canadian emphasis.

broadview press